Oracle Press™

Java EE and HTML5 Enterprise Application Development

ORACLE®　　　*Oracle Press*™

Java EE and HTML5 Enterprise Application Development

John Brock
Arun Gupta
Geertjan Wielenga

New York   Chicago   San Francisco
Athens   London   Madrid   Mexico City
Milan   New Delhi   Singapore   Sydney   Toronto

Cataloging-in-Publication Data is on file with the Library of Congress

1 2 3 4 5 6 7 8 9 0   DOC DOC   1 0 9 8 7 6 5 4

ISBN   978-0-07-182309-8
MHID   0-07-182309-3

Sponsoring Editor	**Technical Editor**	**Production Supervisor**
Brandi Shailer	John Yeary	Jean Bodeaux
Editorial Supervisor	**Copy Editor**	**Composition**
Janet Walden	Bill McManus	Cenveo Publisher Services
Project Manager	**Proofreader**	**Illustration**
Anupriya Tyagi,	Lisa McCoy	Cenveo Publisher Services
Cenveo® Publisher Services	**Indexer**	**Art Director, Cover**
Acquisitions Coordinator	Jack Lewis	Jeff Weeks
Amanda Russell		

*For my wife Lisa: Thanks for encouraging
me to take on this project, and putting up with all the
long nights and mood swings that came with it.*
–John

*To my lovely wife Menka and wonderful boys
Aditya and Mihir for their support and encouragement.*
–Arun

*To my wife Hermine! Also to NetBeans users everywhere—
hope you have fun and learn a lot while you work through this book.*
–Geertjan

About the Authors

John Brock is a Principal Product Manager for Oracle Corporation. John has over 15 years' experience working with web application development. While working at Sun Microsystems, he was responsible for identifying emerging Internet technologies and how they could potentially interact with the Java Virtual Machine (JVM). John has worked with development teams from JRuby, Jython, Groovy, JavaFX, and more. His current focus is on HTML5 application development, and he is the product manager for the HTML5, JavaScript, and CSS3 features of NetBeans IDE. John can easily be reached at @peppertech.

Arun Gupta is Director of Developer Advocacy at Red Hat and focuses on building community around JBoss Middleware. As a founding member of the Java EE team at Sun Microsystems, he spread the love for technology all around the world. At Oracle, Arun led a cross-functional team to drive the global launch of the Java EE 7 platform through strategy, planning, and execution of content, marketing campaigns, and programs. Arun has extensive speaking experience, including appearances in 37 countries speaking on myriad topics, and is a JavaOne Rockstar. An author of a best-selling book, an avid runner, a globe trotter, and a Java Champion, he is easily accessible at @arungupta.

Geertjan Wielenga is a Principal Product Manager for Oracle Corporation. Geertjan has worked in the software industry since 1996. While at Sun Microsystems, he worked on the documentation of a range of technologies, primarily in the Java EE and web areas, developed tutorials, and contributed to published books. Geertjan is a passionate advocate of NetBeans as a central solution to tooling requirements for web-based technologies. He also promotes the NetBeans Platform as a stable and versatile solution for large Java desktop applications. He is currently a product manager assigned to the external evangelism of NetBeans IDE.

About the Technical Editor

John Yeary is a Principal Software Engineer on Epiphany CRM Marketing at Infor Global Solutions. John has been a Java evangelist and has been working with Java since 1995. John is a technical blogger with a focus on Java Enterprise Edition technology, NetBeans, and GlassFish. John is currently the President of the Greenville Java Users Group (GreenJUG), and is its founder. He is an instructor, a mentor, and a prolific open source contributor.

John graduated from Maine Maritime Academy with a B.Sc. Marine Engineering with a concentration in mathematics. He is a Merchant Marine officer, and has a number of licenses and certifications. When he is not doing Java and F/OSS projects, he likes to hike, sail, travel, and spend time with his family. John is also the Assistant Cubmaster in the Boy Scouts of America (BSA) Pack 833, Unit Commissioner, and Southbounder District Chairman for Activities and Civic Service in the Blue Ridge Council of the BSA.

Contents at a Glance

Contents

Acknowledgments

Thanks to Liza Lyons for her help in visualizing the layout of the Book Club sample application. A very big thank you to the editors: from technical to copy. It's amazing what a good editor can do with the chicken scratch of a technical-minded author. It was a joy working with the rest of the Oracle Press team, and, of course, a big thanks to my co-authors.

–John Brock

Sincere thanks to Brandi Shailer and Amanda Russell for shepherding us throughout the process. Many thanks to John Yeary for providing a solid technical review showing his vast knowledge of the subject. This was definitely not possible without my two co-authors and the rest of the team at Oracle Press.

–Arun Gupta

Many thanks to Amanda Russell and Brandi Shailer, as well as JB Brock and Arun Gupta, for the work and cooperation in putting this book together, and to our primary reviewer, John Yeary.

–Geertjan Wielenga

Introduction

Many books are available that cover just Java web services or just HTML5, but not both. So, this book strives to find a balance between what an HTML developer should know about the Java web services they connect to and what the Java developer should know about the HTML5 applications that are consuming and interacting with the web services.

With the resurgence of JavaScript over the past few years, Java developers are often faced with the need to understand how HTML5 client-based applications interact and consume the server-side web services that the developers have been creating. At the same time, HTML5 developers often find that they need to understand how the services their applications rely on are built and configured. With the new HTML5 and CSS3 specifications generating a lot of industry buzz and the new JavaScript libraries, such as AngularJS and Knockout, becoming increasingly popular, some Java developers may wonder whether their skills are still relevant.

Who Should Read This Book

This book is ideal for developers who find that they need to understand not only how to develop Java EE-based web services such as REST, Server-Sent Events (SSE), and WebSocket, but also how to develop HTML5-based clients that consume and interact with those web services. Whether you are primarily a Java developer looking for information about how HTML5 applications connect to your web services, or an HTML5 developer looking to better understand how the Java EE web services are created on the server side, this book will fit your needs.

What This Book Covers

The primary topics covered in this book are

- Java EE 7 Persistence API (JPA)

- Java EE 7 API for RESTful Web Services (JAX-RS)

- Java EE 7 API for WebSocket

- New features of the HTML5 specification

- JavaScript Model-View-ViewModel (MVVM) architectural pattern via Knockout.js

- JavaScript API for REST, WebSocket, and Server-Sent Events (SSE)

- Responsive design concepts via CSS3 features

- CSS preprocessing with Syntactically Awesome StyleSheets (SASS)

- Client and server security concepts for web-based applications

These topics are covered in the following six chapters:

- Chapter 1, "Introduction to Java EE and HTML5 Enterprise Development," provides a brief overview of the three main focus areas of the book: Java EE 7 web services, HTML5 application development, and NetBeans IDE.

- Chapter 2, "Persistence," discusses the Java Persistence API (JPA) and shows you the key concepts for persistence and how data can be created, read, updated, and deleted from a relational database using JPA.

- Chapter 3, "RESTful Resources," introduces you to REST, or Representational State Transfer, as an architectural style for distributed systems such as the World Wide Web. The Java EE 7 API for RESTful Web Services (JAX-RS) is covered, including the new support for Server-Sent Events (SSE). You are shown how to develop your own RESTful web service and SSE service that you will use as the data resources for a Book Club application that you develop in Chapter 5.

■ Chapter 4, "WebSocket," covers the development of both the server and client portions of an application using WebSocket. You learn about the Java API for WebSocket, as well as how to develop an HTML5 client that interacts with the WebSocket service.

■ Chapter 5, "HTML5, JavaScript, and CSS," is all about HTML5 and client-side development. You interact with the REST and SSE web services that you created in Chapter 3. You are shown how to work with the Model-View-ViewModel (MVVM) architectural pattern through the use of the JavaScript library, Knockout. You are introduced to responsive design concepts as well as CSS preprocessing techniques with Syntactically Awesome StyleSheets (SASS).

■ Chapter 6, "HTML5 and Java Application Security," covers security concepts for HTML5 client applications and Java EE–based web services.

How to Use This Book and Code

This book is structured such that you can read it sequentially or jump to any chapter and read it as a stand-alone topic. Source code is provided for all applications discussed in the book and is available for download at www .OraclePressBooks.com. This allows you to start in a later chapter and still have access to the resources that you would have developed had you read the earlier chapters first. For example, if you choose to read Chapter 5 first, in which you develop the Book Club application, you have access to the data resources from Chapter 3 that the application relies on. Download the source code and follow along as you read each chapter, or deploy and run the source code from NetBeans IDE—whichever method works best for you. NetBeans IDE is used throughout the book to show you how to use wizards and other efficient methods of development, such as the built-in JavaScript debugger.

CHAPTER

1

Introduction to Java EE and HTML5 Enterprise Development

There have been many changes taking place in the area of enterprise software development in recent years. Two of the largest changes are the trend toward Software as a Service (SaaS) and the use of HTML5 to provide a pure client-side user interface.

In this chapter, you will be introduced to the main topics that will be covered throughout the book: NetBeans IDE, Java EE 7, and HTML5. You will be presented with information about how to obtain the applications and samples that will help you as you work your way through the coming chapters. Using this combination of IDE, platform, and HTML5 technology, you will soon be building powerful, dynamic enterprise applications.

Development Tools

Three main development tools are used throughout this book: NetBeans IDE, Java EE 7, and HTML5. You will learn how to use the combination of these tools to build powerful, modern enterprise applications. Before you begin building applications, it is important to first make sure you have a solid understanding of the basics of each of these technologies.

NetBeans

NetBeans IDE is the development tool you will use throughout this book. It provides features such as editors, templates, and code generators that make it a perfect fit for creating applications that use Java EE 7 and HTML5. Starting with NetBeans IDE 7.3, new features have been introduced to support and enhance the development experience with client-side web applications that utilize the HTML5 family of technologies. You can use this IDE to rapidly and intuitively create rich web applications that support the responsive web design paradigm targeting desktop and mobile platforms simultaneously. In addition, from NetBeans IDE 7.4 onward, you can use HTML5 technologies within Java EE and PHP applications.

The NetBeans story begins in 1996, when a group of students at Charles University in Prague attempted to write a Delphi-like Java IDE in Java. Originally called Xelfi, the student project delved into what was then the uncharted territory of Java IDEs. Xelfi generated enough interest in the developer community that, after they graduated, the students decided to put their new product on the market. In 1997, they formed a company and changed the name of the IDE to NetBeans.

It wasn't long before Sun Microsystems became interested in NetBeans as Sun began searching for Java development tools. In 1999, Sun acquired NetBeans and made the NetBeans IDE the flagship toolset for Java. At the time, Sun made another critical decision: to establish NetBeans IDE as an open source project—free to anyone who wanted to use it. Over the years, the NetBeans IDE has become a fully featured, cross-platform IDE, supporting all aspects of Java application development.

When Oracle acquired Sun in 2010, NetBeans IDE became part of Oracle, and Oracle made the commitment to continue to support it. Today, more people are using NetBeans IDE than ever before. By 2010, the one million active user mark was reached, and the NetBeans IDE community continues to innovate and grow.

You can download NetBeans IDE from the Oracle NetBeans website. Visit http://netbeans.org/downloads for an overview of the available distributions and to find the corresponding download links. You need to have either the "Java EE" or "All" distribution of NetBeans IDE to be able to follow the instructions in this book. The instructions and code samples have been created in NetBeans IDE 7.4, the latest version at the time of writing. Subsequently released versions of NetBeans IDE should work just as well, though if you encounter problems when using a later version, you are recommended to switch to NetBeans IDE 7.4.

Having just the Java Runtime Environment (JRE) installed on your system is not sufficient for running NetBeans IDE. You need to have the Java Development Kit (JDK), which includes a copy of the JRE. The IDE relies on development tools and sources provided by the JDK. You can go to http://oracle.com/technetwork/java/index.html to find and download the latest version of the JDK.

Java EE 7

Java Platform, Enterprise Edition (Java EE) provides a standards-based platform for developing web and enterprise applications. The platform consists of multiple components that enable developers to build these applications. Each component is defined using a formal specification that describes the

proposed component and its features. The platform is also accompanied by an application programming interface (API) described using *Javadoc*. This API is then used to build the application. The platform also provides some additional services, such as naming, injection, and resource management, that span across the platform. These applications are then deployed in Java EE 7 containers, such as GlassFish, that provide the runtime support.

There are 33 components defined in the Java EE 7 platform. The ones that are pertinent to the content of this book are described in this section. For a full list of the components, refer to *The Java EE 7 Technologies* list (www.oracle.com/technetwork/java/javaee/tech/index.html).

One of the major themes for the Java EE 7 platform is to simplify development of HTML5 applications, especially the services that are needed on the server side. To enable that, Java API for RESTful Web Services (JAX-RS) is a component in the platform that defines how to develop, deploy, and invoke RESTful Web Services. A Plain Old Java Object (POJO) can be easily published as a Representational State Transfer (REST) endpoint by specifying an annotation. Regular methods can be easily invoked when the resource is accessed using standard HTTP verbs. A standard Java API to invoke these REST endpoints is also available. Server-Sent Events (SSE), a key part of the HTML5 specification, is used to asynchronously push data from the server to the client. Even though SSE is not part of the platform yet, the JAX-RS implementation provides support for SSE.

WebSocket provides a full-duplex, bidirectional communication channel over a single TCP connection and significantly improves the latency for modern web applications. A new API was added to the Java EE 7 platform for building WebSocket applications. Just like JAX-RS, adding an annotation on a POJO converts it into a WebSocket endpoint. With all the excitement around WebSocket and a simplified API, Java EE 7 is the best platform for building your HTML5 applications.

JavaScript Object Notation (JSON) is a key technology for data transfer within HTML5 applications, and certainly a lingua franca of the Web. Java EE 7 adds new APIs to enable the parsing and generation of JSON text and objects using JSON-P 1.0. The API allows parsing or generating the entire JSON text using only the API. Alternatively, the document may be structured one item at a time.

Any web application typically requires information to be persisted in a permanent data store. The Java Persistence API (JPA) defines an API for the management of persistence and object-relational mapping using a

Java domain model. Consistent with the overarching theme of a simplified programming model, adding an annotation allows a POJO to be mapped to a database table. There are reasonable defaults that can be overridden using annotations. The POJOs can also be used to generate the database tables, or even table-generation scripts. Developers can write string-based or type-safe queries to operate on the Java data model.

In addition, the information from this data store needs to be stored and retrieved to preserve the ACID (atomicity, consistency, isolation, durability) properties. This can be achieved using Enterprise JavaBeans (EJB) or the newly introduced @Transactional annotation. EJBs provide convenient container-managed transactions. They also come in different flavors: stateless (where there is no state on the server), stateful (state is stored on the server), and singleton (single instance per application per JVM).

The newly added @Transactional annotation can be specified on a POJO to provide container-managed transactions outside of Enterprise JavaBeans. Annotating a class means all methods of the class are going to run inside a container-managed transaction. Alternatively, this annotation may be specified on a method to limit the scope of transaction.

This book will cover all of these topics in detail using extensive code samples.

In addition, the Java EE 7 platform provides several other components:

- **Batch Applications for the Java Platform**   Allows noninteractive, bulk-oriented, and long-running tasks to be easily defined and executed. It allows item-oriented processing style, aka *Chunk*, and task-oriented processing style, aka *Batchlet*. Chunk, the primary and recommended processing style, reads, processes, and aggregates for writing a "chunk" number of items at a time. Each chunk is written in a container-managed transaction and also provides checkpoints. Batchlet is a roll-your-own batch pattern. It is a task-oriented processing style where a task is invoked once, runs to completion, and returns an exit status.

- **Java Message Service (JMS)**   Provides a message-oriented middleware that allows sending and receiving messages between distributed systems. It provides a *point-to-point* messaging model, where a publisher sends a message to a specific destination, called a *queue*, targeted to a subscriber. Alternatively, JMS provides a *publish-subscribe* messaging model where multiple publishers can publish a message to a destination, called a *topic*, which can then be subscribed to by multiple subscribers. In both cases, publisher and subscriber are loosely coupled from each other. They only need to know the destination and message format.

■ **Contexts and Dependency Injection (CDI)** Provides a type-safe dependency injection mechanism. A bean is "strongly typed" as it only defines the type and semantics of other beans it depends upon, without a string name and using the type information available in the Java type system. It provides "loose coupling" as the injection request need not be aware of the actual life cycle, concrete implementation, threading model, or other clients of the bean.

■ **Concurrency Utilities** Allows adding concurrency design principles for existing Java EE applications. It allows an application to create user threads that are managed by the container. The usual classloading context, Java Naming and Directory Interface (JNDI) context, and security context are propagated to these threads.

■ **JavaServer Faces (JSF)** Provides the server-side user interface (UI) framework. It allows creation of web pages with a set of reusable UI components following the Model-View-Controller (MVC) design pattern. The components are bound to a server-side model that enables two-way migration of application data with the UI. JSF also defines page navigation, manages UI component state across server requests, and can be easily used to build and reuse custom components.

■ **Java Servlet Technology** Allows a web client to interact using a request/response pattern and generates dynamic content. The container is responsible for the life cycle of the servlet, receives requests and sends responses, and performs any other encoding/decoding required as part of that function.

Refer to *The Java EE 7 Tutorial* (http://docs.oracle.com/javaee/7/tutorial/doc/home.htm) for more details on the complete set of Java EE 7 technologies.

HTML5

HTML

While most people believe HTML5 is relatively new, it has actually been in development since 2004. The World Wide Web Consortium (W3C) designed the original specification to address what it observed as common uses of HTML and XHTML across the Internet at the time. Other considerations the W3C addressed as it drafted the new specification were the trend toward incorporating multimedia into web pages and the need to consolidate various specifications that had become commonly used during the years that the HTML 4.01 specification had been in use. This consolidation included not only upgrading to the HTML 4 specification, but also combining the XHTML 1 and DOM Level 2 HTML specifications into one.

HTML5 Specification Reaches Feature Complete

What has brought HTML5 to the forefront the most over the past year is that on December 17, 2012, the W3C announced that the HTML5 specification was feature complete. By labeling the specification as a "Candidate Recommendation," the W3C gave businesses and developers a stable specification that they could start working with.

One major issue that you need to take into consideration when working with HTML5 as your client-side application framework is that, while it has reached a stable, feature-complete status, it has not been approved as a completed standard yet. The largest ramification of this is that there are still different implementations of what was a draft specification being used. Now that the specification is feature complete, the major browser vendors and user agent developers should be able to converge on implementations that come closer to meeting the specification. This will take time though, and you will need to make sure you test all of your HTML5 code on the browsers and user agents that you expect your customers to be using.

In its press release announcing the completed definition of the HTML5 specification (www.w3.org/2012/12/html5-cr.html.en), the W3C describes as follows what the next phase of the specification process will involve:

> During this stage, the W3C HTML Working Group will conduct a variety of activities to ensure that the specifications may be implemented compatibly across browsers, authoring tools, email clients, servers, content management systems, and other Web tools. The group will

analyze current HTML5 implementations, establish priorities for test development, and work with the community to develop those tests. The HTML Working Group has planned for this implementation phase to last into mid-2014, after which W3C expects to publish the final HTML5 Recommendation, available Royalty-Free to implementers under the W3C Patent Policy.

The implementation of the HTML5 specification so far has been done against a moving target, so to speak. Different vendors support the specification in different ways, or may not support certain parts of the specification at all. This poses a problem for application developers, who have to develop for a customer base that could be using a wide variety of device and browser combinations. Thankfully, several websites have been created to help developers navigate this tricky area of developing HTML applications. Two of the more popular sites are

- **HTML5 Test** http://html5test.com/

- **Can I Use** http://caniuse.com/

The HTML5 Test website will allow you to see how well a specific version or brand of browser implements the whole of the HTML5 specification. This is very useful when you are trying to decide what kind of browser or device support matrix your application will provide.

The Can I Use website goes into more detail and allows you to look at a specific HTML element or attribute and see which browser vendors have implemented it and in which versions of their browsers.

Use of Mobile Devices

Probably the second largest reason for HTML5's recent rise in visibility is the increase in the availability of smartphones, tablets, and other types of mobile and embedded devices with Internet access (such as Internet-ready TVs, game consoles, and Blu-ray players, to name just a few). The reason that the rise in the availability of these devices has brought HTML5 to prominence is that all of them are being developed with browsers that already support HTML5 to some degree. Unlike on desktop operating systems, the developers of the browsers for these devices didn't have to consider any issues of backward compatibility with existing browser implementations. Everything is new on these types of devices, and the manufacturers started with the latest HTML specifications in anticipation of it becoming the standard in the near future.

This rise in accessing the Internet via mobile devices is also one of the factors that has enticed enterprise developers to look more closely at HTML5. The traditional website layout does not comfortably scale down for viewing on a smaller device like a smartphone or tablet. The existing methods of producing a completely different version of the website to display when the client is detected to be a mobile device have proven to be fraught with maintenance problems and inefficient to scale.

New HTML5 Features

One of the major new features of HTML5 is the inclusion of new semantic elements (see Table 1-1) to help developers manage the layout of the HTML page and its content so that it scales flawlessly for viewing on smaller devices. You can now lay out your HTML content using tags such as <header>, <footer>, <section>, <article>, <aside>, <nav>, and many others.

Along with the new semantic elements in the HTML5 specification, there are also new syntactic elements, as listed in Table 1-2, that are meant to

Element	Description
<header>	The header section of a document. Usually contains introductory or navigational information.
<footer>	The footer of a document. Usually contains things like copyright information, legal information, links to more information about the website, etc.
<section>	A generic section in a document.
<article>	An independent area of content within the document.
<aside>	A piece of content that is only slightly connected to the rest of the document.
<main>	The main content for the document. Only one of these elements is allowed in the document.
<dialog>	A section of the document that will be used as a dialog box or pop-up window.
<nav>	A section of the document meant for navigation links.
<menuitem>	A piece of text that represents a command the user can choose from a pop-up menu.

(Continued)

TABLE 1-1.   *Semantic Elements*

Element	Description
<mark>	A piece of text that should be highlighted for reference.
<details>	A section of the document that contains additional controls or information that can be shown or hidden on demand.
<summary>	Provides the summary content for the <details> element.
<bdi>	A section of the document that needs to be isolated from other parts because it might be formatted for languages that need bidirectional language support.
<figure>	A self-contained section of the document having its own flow. Usually of a graphical nature, such as images, video content, etc.
<figcaption>	A caption for a <figure> element.
<meter>	A section of the document that represents a measurement.
<progress>	A section that presents the completion of a task.
<ruby>	Allows for the inclusion of Ruby annotations. Usually used in East Asian typography.
<rt>	Subelement of <ruby>.
<rp>	Subelement of <ruby>.
<time>	An element containing date and/or time information.
<wbr>	An opportunity for a line break.
<datalist>	Used in conjunction with the list attribute of an <input> element to create combo boxes.
<output>	A section of the document that represents the output of some kind of calculation.
<keygen>	Used as a key pair generator control.

TABLE 1-1. *Semantic Elements*

remove the need to install proprietary plug-ins. These include elements such as <canvas>, <video>, <audio>, and <svg>. These features are designed to make it easier to work with multimedia and graphics.

Lastly, the HTML5 specification brings new attributes to some of the existing elements. The most notable of these are the new values for the type attributes of the <input> element (see Table 1-3). These are primarily used for forms. While all of these new type values are now part of the finalized

Element	Description
<audio>	Audio multimedia content.
<video>	Video multimedia content.
<source>	A subelement of both <audio> and <video>. Used when there are multiple source formats available.
<track>	Text tracks for the <video> element.
<canvas>	A section used for rendering dynamic bitmap content. Intended for content like graphs or games.
<svg>	A section used for rendering Scalable Vector Graphics (SVG).

TABLE 1-2.   *Syntactic Elements*

Attribute	Description
<input type="color"/>	Input field value represents a color
<input type="date"/>	Input field value represents a date
<input type="datetime"/>	Input field value represents a date and time
<input type="datetime-local"/>	Input field value represents a local date and time with no time-zone offset
<input type="time"/>	Input field value represents a time
<input type="email"/>	Input field value represents an email address
<input type="month"/>	Input field value represents a month
<input type="week"/>	Input field value represents a week
<input type="number"/>	Input field value represents a number
<input type="range"/>	Input field value represents a range between a minimum and maximum setting
<input type="search"/>	Input field value represents a search
<input type="tel"/>	Input field value represents a telephone number
<input type="url"/>	Input field value represents a URL

TABLE 1-3.   *Form Input Type Attributes*

HTML5 specification, each browser vendor can, and has, implemented how they behave when they are rendered. It is the intent of the specification that the vendor will be able to provide a user interface for better integration with each of these input types. For instance, if a browser renders an input field with the type set to `"date"`, the end user would see a date picker displayed to help select the date that they wish to enter. Unfortunately, this is one of the areas in which browser vendors currently have the largest separation in functionality. On mobile devices, the experience is better. You will often find that when you click or touch in an input field that has the type set to `"number"`, you will get a number pad instead of the normal keyboard, or a different type of keyboard will be displayed if the input field is set to something like `"url"`.

Parts of an HTML5 Application

One of the most common misconceptions about HTML5 applications is that they are composed of HTML5 only. In fact, in almost all cases the application is actually made up of at least three different components: HTML5, JavaScript, and Cascading Style Sheets (CSS). By combining all of the new HTML5 elements and attributes with the new media query feature of CSS version 3 (CSS3), you can display the same content with different layouts for different device sizes. This method of modifying the content to respond to the device's available display size is called *responsive design*; the layout responds to the display size that it is rendered in.

There are a few important caveats to note about responsive design. First, although it does allow you to create a website that will have the same look and feel across multiple device sizes, the HTML5 application is still a web page that is being viewed in a web browser on a smaller device such as a smartphone or tablet. The application will not have a true "native" look and feel like an application that is written and compiled for a specific type of mobile device. Second, HTML5 and responsive design may not be the answer for developers who want their application to have access to specific mobile features such as the camera, contact list, and calendar. Because the application is running in a web browser, you can only program your application to use what the browser allows you to interact with.

As previously mentioned, the third component commonly used in HTML5 applications is JavaScript. The introduction of JavaScript architectural libraries has been a big factor in making it more acceptable to enterprise developers.

Developing an application in an enterprise environment often means the separation of development tasks, with designers and UI teams working on the front end or view layer, while other teams are working on the data and controller layers. This type of separation between application layers is referred to as a Model-View-Controller (MVC) architectural pattern. Over the past few years, JavaScript libraries have been developed to introduce a similar architecture, called Model-View-ViewModel (MVVM).

MVVM was originally developed by Microsoft in 2005 as part of its Windows Presentation Foundation (WPF). A JavaScript implementation of this architectural pattern was introduced as an open source project in 2010 by Steve Sanderson. It was released under the name of Knockout.js (http://knockoutjs .com/) and has quickly gained popularity among JavaScript developers who are already familiar with the MVC architectural development practices. While a deep understanding of MVVM, and more specifically Knockout.js, is beyond the scope of this book, you will use Knockout.js in Chapter 5 when creating an HTML5 application that will consume and interact with web services such as REST, WebSockets, and Server-Sent Events (SSE).

Summary

You've learned what's new in the Java EE 7 specification in the area of web services that are used for developing the specific services that an HTML5 application will need. You've also been shown some of the new features in the HTML5 specification and the specific technologies that are required to develop a client-side HTML5 application. This introduction to the current state of development tools will help you throughout the rest of this book as you work with the coding concepts and samples.

As you can see, both Java EE web development and HTML web development have matured over the past few years toward the common trend of providing Software as a Service. In keeping with this development trend, tools such as NetBeans IDE have evolved to provide features that make it easier than ever to combine these two types of technologies.

In the next chapter, you will dive into the Java EE 7 Persistence API to learn how to create and maintain a data store for your HTML5 application.

CHAPTER
2

Persistence

Data is an integral part of any application and typically defines the state of an application at any given point of time. *Persistence* is the characteristic of an application state that outlives the process that created it. Absent persistence, application data would be lost when the application terminates. If a banking application could not persist information about the accounts, that application would be useless. Similarly, if a retail store application could not persist information about the inventory, customer orders, and shipments, it would be of no value. Persistence allows applications to access the data and perform CRUD (create, read, update, and delete) operations that change the data's state. After an application crashes unexpectedly and then recovers, persistence enables the application to use the data in the exact state that it was in at the time of the crash.

There are many ways to persist data in Java. Java Platform, Standard Edition (Java SE) provides APIs to manipulate streams and files. This requires lots of low-level handling, such as defining the stream location and names, opening and closing streams, and defining a data format. The Java Database Connectivity (JDBC) API can be used to store data to a relational database such as an Oracle or MySQL database server. This requires managing database connections, writing SQL queries, mapping results with Java objects, and a lot more. Different NoSQL data stores provide APIs to manage data specific to those data stores. The majority of data is persisted in databases, specifically relational databases.

The Java EE platform provides the Java Persistence API (JPA) for the management of persistence and object/relational mapping. In other words, a POJO (Plain Old Java Object) can be used to represent a table in the relational database, and each class instance corresponds to a row in that table. The API defines how these rows can be managed using the POJO.

Data stored in a relational database should maintain ACID (atomicity, consistency, isolation, durability) properties. To help ensure that ACID properties are maintained, it is very important to ensure that any addition, update, or deletion of data is done within a transactional boundary. The transactions can be *container-managed* or *user-managed*. Container-managed transactions can be managed either by the Enterprise JavaBeans (EJB) container or by using the @javax.transaction.Transactional annotation provided by the Java Transaction API (JTA). In this case, a transaction is automatically started by the container and then either committed or rolled back by the container. A user-managed transaction is explicitly started and completed by the user. In this case, the application explicitly starts the transaction and then either commits or rolls back the transaction before exiting out of the method.

This chapter will introduce the main concepts of JPA, how an entity can be created, queried, and updated. Text-based Java Persistence Query Language (JPQL) and type-safe Criteria API are explained. Container-managed transactions that preserve the ACID properties of these entities are explained. Finally, database schema generation using persistence properties is explained. NetBeans IDE tools and wizards are explained in reference to context throughout the chapter.

JPA Entity

JPA defines an *entity* as a lightweight persistent domain object. Any POJO with a no-args public constructor can be defined as an entity. A JPA entity defining the concept of an author is shown in Listing 2-1.

Listing 2-1   *Author Entity*

```
@Entity
@Table(name = "AUTHOR")
public class Author implements Serializable {
    private static final long serialVersionUID = 1L;
    @Id
    @NotNull
    private Integer id;

    @NotNull
    @Size(min = 1, max = 20)
    private String firstName;

    @Size(max = 20)
    private String lastName;

    @Size(max = 1000)
    private String bio;

    @Size(max = 30)
    private String email;
    public Author() { }
    // other convenience constructors

    // getters and setters
}
```

Let us walk through this code:

■ `@javax.persistence.Entity` annotation on a POJO specifies that this is an entity. The default name of the entity is the unqualified name of the class. An optional `name` attribute may be used to specify the entity name, which is then used to refer to the entity in queries.

■ `@javax.persistence.Table` is an optional annotation on an entity and specifies the primary table for the annotated entity. Additional tables may be specified using `SecondaryTable` or `SecondaryTables` annotation.

If no `@Table` annotation is specified on the entity, or the annotation is specified but no `name` attribute is specified, then the generated table defaults to the entity name.

■ Implementing the `Serializable` interface allows the class to be passed by value through a remote interface.

■ The properties of the bean that follow the JavaBeans-style accessors ("property access") or instance variables ("field access") represent the persistent state of the entity. The persistent fields or properties of an entity class can be from a wide range of types, such as Java primitive types, any primitive wrapper type, other fine-grained classes defined using `@javax.persistence.Embedded` and known as *embeddables,* a collection of embeddables, and many other types.

The properties `id`, `firstName`, `lastName`, `bio`, and `email` have getters and setters that are omitted for brevity in this code. Each of these fields will map to a column in the database table.

Reasonable default column names are used for properties and fields. For example, the column name `ID` is used for the `id` property, and the column name `FIRST_NAME` is used for the `firstName` property. Optionally, a `@javax.persistence.Column` annotation may be used to override the name of the mapped column. This annotation can also use several attributes to control the definition of the mapped column.

■ `@javax.persistence.Id` annotation specifies the primary key of an entity. The field or property to which this annotation is applied should be one of the following types: any Java primitive type, any primitive wrapper type, `java.lang.String`, `java.util.Date`, `java.sql.Date`, `java.math.BigDecimal`, or `java.math` `.BigInteger`. The corresponding mapped column is assumed to be the primary key of the primary table.

A composite primary key that consists of multiple fields or properties can be defined using @`javax.persistence.IdClass` annotation on an entity. An embeddable class can be denoted as the primary key using @`javax.persistence.EmbeddedId` annotation.

■ Validation constraints can be specified on entities to ensure that only valid data is used to communicate with the database. Bean Validation 1.1, another specification in the Java EE 7 platform, defines several such predefined constraints in the `javax.validation.constraints` package. Specifying @`javax.validation.constraints` `.NotNull` on a field ensures that this field cannot be set to `null` and persisted. The @`javax.validation.constraints.Size` constraint allows you to specify minimum and maximum boundaries of the field.

The Bean Validation specification even defines an extensible mechanism by which you can easily define custom constraints to meet application needs.

An entity can capture the relationship between different tables using @javax.persistence.OneToOne, @javax.persistence.OneToMany, @javax.persistence.ManyToOne, and @javax.persistence .ManyToMany annotations. A join table is defined using @javax.persistence .JoinTable annotation. A collection of basic or embeddable types can be mapped using @javax.persistence.CollectionTable annotation.

NetBeans IDE provides a wizard that enables you to generate JPA entities from a database schema. In the IDE, right-click your application and choose New | Other | Persistence | Entity Classes from Database. The Database Tables page of the New Entity Classes from Database wizard is shown in Figure 2-1. The tables available in the selected data source are displayed in the Available Tables list.

Select any tables in the Available Tables list in the left pane and click the Add button to add them to the Selected Tables list on the right. If you add a table that references other tables, the referenced tables are automatically added to the Selected Tables list as well. The referenced tables are grayed out

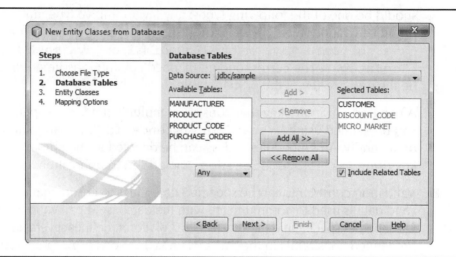

FIGURE 2-1. *Selecting tables from a database*

to indicate that they are referenced tables. The IDE will automatically generate entity classes for each of the tables listed in the Selected Tables list.

Click Next to move to the Entity Classes page of the New Entity Classes from Database wizard, as shown in Figure 2-2, where you review or set the following:

- **Class Names** Displays the name of the class that is generated for each table listed. The Generation Type column displays whether the class will be new, updated, or re-created. If the entity class for a selected table already exists, you can choose to either re-create the entity class or update the existing class by clicking the toggle button (...) below the Class Names table.

- **Project** Displays the project where the entity classes will be saved. This field is read-only.

- **Location** Select the source folder where you want to create the entity class.

- **Package** Select an existing package from the drop-down list or type the name of a new package.

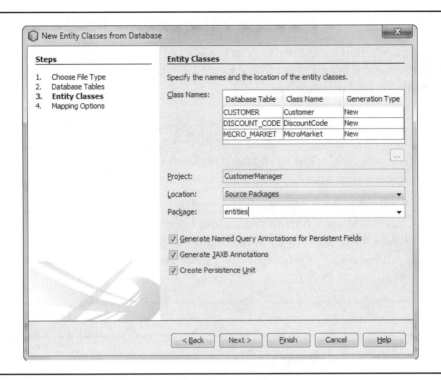

FIGURE 2-2. *Defining classes and other files to be created*

- **Generate Named Query Annotations for Persistent Fields** If selected, the IDE generates named query annotations in the entity classes.

- **Generate JAXB Annotations** If selected, the IDE generates annotations in the entity class for mapping the class to an XML element that can then be used by a Java Architecture for XML Binding (JAXB) web service.

To persist entity classes, your project requires a persistence unit (as described in the following section, "Packaging an Entity"). NetBeans IDE checks if there is a persistence unit for the project when you create the entity class. If the IDE cannot locate a persistence unit, the Create Persistence Unit check box appears, as shown in Figure 2-2. Alternatively, you can create a persistence unit later by choosing Persistence | Persistence Unit in the New File wizard.

From the Entity Classes page, you can click Finish to create entity classes for each of the specified tables, or you can click Next to modify the default settings used when generating the mapping annotations, as shown in Figure 2-3. If you choose the latter option, you can set the following options for configuring generated annotation elements:

- **Association Fetch**   Select the fetch element to add to the relationship annotations. You can select default, eager, or lazy. If default is selected (default is selected by default), no fetch element is added to the relationship annotations.

- **Collection Type**   Select the collection type for OneToMany and ManyToMany Container-Managed Relationship (CMR) fields. You can select `java.util.Collection`, `java.util.List`, or `java.util.Set`. `java.util.Collection` is selected by default.

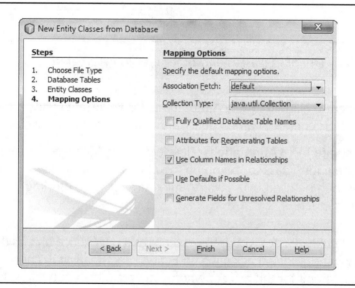

FIGURE 2-3.   *Setting options for the creation of entity classes*

- **Fully Qualified Database Table Names**   If selected, `catalog` and `schema` elements are added to the `@Table` annotation. This option is deselected by default.

- **Attributes for Regenerating Database Tables**   If selected, `nullable` (when it is false), `length` (for String type), `precision`, and `scale` (for decimal type) are added to the `@Column` annotation. Unique constraints are also added to the `@Table` annotation if this option is selected. This option is deselected by default.

- **Use Column Names in Relationships**   If selected, when a table references a foreign key, the field name is generated according to the name of the column in the table. For example, if the table `customer` has a column named `zip` that is mapped to a column named `zip_code` in table `micromarket`, the generated field name will be `zip`. This option is selected by default.

  If this option is deselected, the field name is generated according to the name of the table that contains the foreign key. In the example shown in the previous figures, the generated field name will be `microMarket`.

- **Use Defaults if Possible**   If selected, only annotations that modify the default behavior or attributes will be generated. Selecting this option can reduce the number of unnecessary annotations that are generated. This option is deselected by default.

- **Generate Fields for Unresolved Relationships**   If selected, basic generic fields are generated for the fields in a relationship that reference fields or entities that are missing or cannot be resolved. The basic fields that are generated might not accurately represent the columns in the tables because of the missing data.

  If this option is deselected, fields in a relationship are not generated if any of the fields or entities in the relationship are missing. This option is deselected by default.

When you click Finish, the IDE creates entity classes for each of the tables you specified in the wizard, as shown in Figure 2-4.

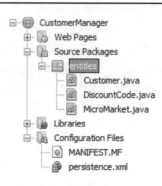

FIGURE 2-4. *Examining the result of creating new entity classes*

Packaging an Entity

An entity is managed within a *persistence context*, a set of managed entity instances in which any persistent entity identity has a unique entity instance. A persistence context has multiple *entity managers* that manage the entity instances and their life cycles. The entity managers, their configuration information, the managed entities, and optional metadata that defines the mapping of the entities to the database are together packaged as a *persistence unit*. A persistence unit is defined by a `persistence .xml` file and packaged within a WAR file. Listing 2-2 shows a sample `persistence.xml` file.

Listing 2-2 *Sample persistence.xml File*

```
<?xml version="1.0" encoding="UTF-8"?>
<persistence version="2.1" xmlns="http://xmlns.jcp.org/xml/ns/
persistence " xmlns:xsi="http://www.w3.org/2001/XMLSchema-instance"
xsi:schemaLocation="http://xmlns.jcp.org/xml/ns/persistence http://
xmlns.jcp.org/xml/ns/persistence/persistence_2_1.xsd ">
    <persistence-unit name="authorPU" transaction-type="JTA">
        <properties>
        </properties>
    </persistence-unit>
</persistence>
```

The persistence.xml file can have one or more <persistence-unit> elements, each corresponding to an entity manager. Each entity manager can be configured using several standard javax.persistence.* <properties> elements.

NetBeans IDE provides an editor for editing persistence.xml files. Open a persistence.xml file and you will see that three different views are available for working with the file: Design, Source, and History. Click the Source button to see the source of the file. When you use code completion in Source view—that is, you press CTRL-TAB (by default)—context-sensitive suggestions are shown for completing the current word, together with relevant documentation, as shown in Figure 2-5.

When you click the Design button, a structured view is shown for working with the persistence.xml file (see Figure 2-6). A drop-down list lets you navigate to sections of interest, while text fields and buttons let you enter values into the underlying persistence.xml file.

Finally, clicking the History button opens a local history view of your file. The History view lets you roll back changes that are saved locally.

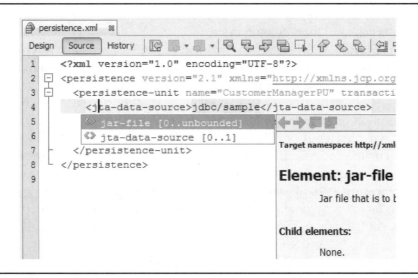

FIGURE 2-5. *Source view for persistence.xml file*

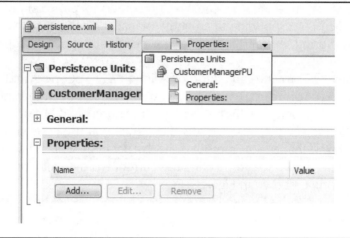

FIGURE 2-6. *Design view for persistence.xml file*

Managing an Entity

Each entity goes through create, read, update, and delete (CRUD) operations during its life cycle. Typically, an entity is created once, read and updated multiple times, and then deleted once.

An Enterprise JavaBean (EJB; also known as *enterprise beans*) is typically used to manage the entity. An EJB instance is itself managed at runtime by an EJB container. The container provides all the plumbing, such as transactions, remoting, concurrency, connection pooling, and other such details, so that the application developer can focus on the business logic.

There are two types of EJBs: session beans and message-driven beans. A session bean processes the message synchronously, and a message-driven bean is used to process messages asynchronously. There are three types of session beans: stateful, stateless, and singleton. A *stateful* session bean maintains a conversational state for a specific client, a *stateless* session bean does not contain any conversational state for a specific client, and a *singleton* session bean is instantiated once per application.

A stateless session bean, by its very nature of being stateless, can be pooled by the container and provides much better scalability for the application. By default, all methods of a session bean have container-managed transactions. This means the EJB container implements all the low-level transaction protocols, such as the two-phase commit protocol between a transaction manager and a database system, to honor the transactional semantics. The changes to the underlying resources are all committed or rolled back accordingly.

A container-managed entity manager can be obtained in a stateless session bean using dependency injection. The entity manager is then used to perform operations on an entity.

Listing 2-3 shows how a stateless session bean can be used to create or delete an entity instance.

Listing 2-3   *CRUDing Author Entity*

```
@Stateless
public class AuthorSessionBean {
    @PersistenceContext
    EntityManager em;
    public void addAuthor(Author e) {
      em.persist(e);
    }
    public void deleteAuthor(Author e) {
      em.remove(e);
    }
}
```

A stateless session bean is defined by adding @javax.ejb.Stateless annotation on a POJO. To create a new row in the database table, a new entity instance is created using a no-args constructor or a convenience constructor. Calling setters or assigning instance variables then populates the entity values. This is typically done in a client component such as a servlet or any other Java EE component.

A container-managed javax.persistence.EntityManager is obtained and used within the addAuthor() method to save the entity. Similarly, an entity instance can be removed by calling the EntityManager .remove() method. The EJB container starts a transaction before the method is invoked and commits the transaction after the method completes. All changes made to the entity manager are stored in the database with a transaction commit.

NetBeans IDE provides a wizard that enables you to generate EJBs. In the IDE, right-click your application and choose New | Other | Enterprise JavaBeans | Session Bean to open the New Session Bean wizard, shown in Figure 2-7.

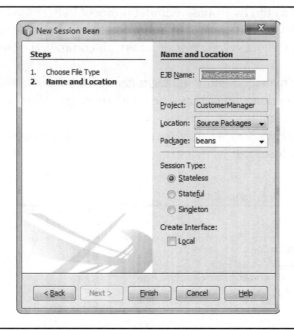

FIGURE 2-7. *Creating new session beans*

For Session Type, you can select one of the following:

■ **Stateless**   The bean does not save state information during its
  conversation with the user. These enterprise beans are useful for
  simple interactions between the client and the application service,
  interactions that are complete in a single method invocation.
  An example is an enterprise bean that processes orders. Each
  order can be processed by an invocation of one method, such as
  `processOrder()`. All the information needed for processing is
  contained in the method parameters.

■ **Stateful**   The bean saves state information during its conversation
  with the user. These enterprise beans are useful for business
  processes that require an interaction between a client and application
  service that lasts longer than a single method invocation and requires
  memory of the state of the interaction. An example is an online
  shopping cart. The end user, through the client program, can order a

number of items. The stateful session bean managing the interaction must accumulate items until the end user is ready to review the accumulated order, approve or reject items, and initiate processing of the lot. The stateful session bean has to store the unprocessed items and enable the end user to add more.

■ **Singleton**   A singleton session bean is instantiated only once per application and exists for the life cycle of the application. You can create a singleton bean that the container instantiates when the application starts up by using the @Startup annotation. An example is a bean that is used to initialize data for an application that can be concurrently accessed by many clients.

An alternative to using an EJB container providing container-managed transactions is to use the newly introduced @javax.transaction .Transactional annotation on a POJO or its method. This allows declarative definition of transaction boundaries on beans managed by Contexts and Dependency Injection (CDI), as well as classes defined as managed beans or other Java EE components. The transactional semantics are implemented using CDI interceptor bindings.

Listing 2-4 shows how @javax.transaction.Transactional annotation can be specified on a method to create or delete an entity instance. Just like in EJB, a container-managed transaction is automatically started by the CDI runtime and committed or rolled back, as appropriate.

Listing 2-4   *Author with @Transactional*

```
public class AuthorSessionBean {
    @PersistenceContext
    EntityManager em;

    @Transactional
    public void addAuthor(Author e) {
      em.persist(e);
    }

    @Transactional
    public void deleteAuthor(Author e) {
      em.remove(e);
    }
}
```

Java Persistence Query Language

Java Persistence Query Language (JPQL) is a string-based query language used to define queries over entities and their persistent state. JPQL allows the application developer to specify the semantics of queries in a portable way. The underlying persistence provider converts the query language to a target language, such as SQL, of a database or a persistent store.

A query may be a SELECT statement (*R* from Read of CRUD), UPDATE statement (*U* from Update of CRUD), or DELETE statement (*D* from Delete of CRUD). An optional WHERE clause can be used to restrict the results, and a GROUP BY clause, HAVING clause, or ORDER BY clause can be used to aggregate the results. The query may be constructed dynamically or may be statically defined in a metadata annotation.

As shown in the following example, `@javax.persistence` `.NamedQueries` annotation can be used on an entity to specify multiple named JPQL queries. Each query is specified using `@javax.persistence` `.NamedQuery` annotation. Each query requires a `name` attribute to uniquely identify the query within the persistence unit. The query string is defined using the `query` attribute.

```
@NamedQueries({
    @NamedQuery(name = " Author.findAll", query = " SELECT a FROM
Author a"),
    @NamedQuery(name = " Author.findById", query = "SELECT a FROM
Author a WHERE a.id = :id")
})
```

In the preceding example, both the queries are statically defined. The first query has the name `Author.findAll` and is equivalent to selecting all rows from the table. Note that the query string is defined around the entity, and not the corresponding database table. This is what provides portability of JPQL over multiple databases. The second query has the name `Author.findById`, uses a WHERE clause to restrict the result set, and requires a parameter `id` to be specified.

NetBeans IDE provides a JPQL Query dialog so that you can verify queries without deploying the application. Before you use it, make sure to compile the JPA entities in your application, since these compiled classes are used by the JPQL Query dialog. Then, as shown in Figure 2-8, right-click

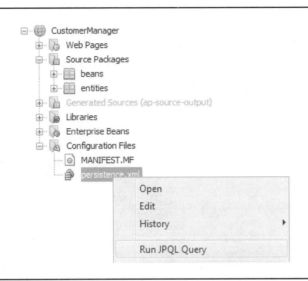

FIGURE 2-8.   *Opening the JPQL Query dialog*

the `persistence.xml` file and choose Run JPQL Query to open the JPQL Query dialog.

In the JPQL Query dialog, you can use code completion, CTRL-TAB (by default), to help you define your queries. When you run a query, the results are shown in the Result tab, as shown in Figure 2-9, while the SQL version of the query is available in the SQL tab.

Criteria API

The `javax.persistence.Criteria` API is an object-based, type-safe alternative to string-based JPQL. It operates on a metamodel of the entities, which is typically generated by an annotation processor. The metamodel is a set of classes that describes your domain model and provides a generic way to deal with an application's domain model. The APIs in the package, `javax.persistence.criteria` and `javax.persistence.metamodel`, are used to create this strongly typed query.

Listing 2-5 shows how you can write the `Author.findAll` query using the `Criteria` API.

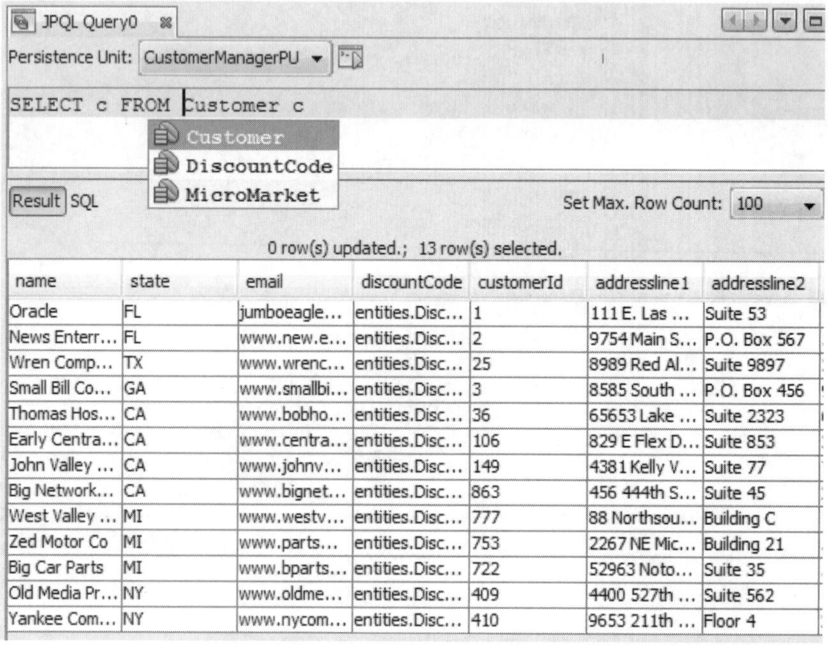

FIGURE 2-9. *Showing query results*

Listing 2-5 *Author Criteria Query*

```
CriteriaBuilder builder = em.getCriteriaBuilder();
CriteriaQuery criteria = builder.createQuery (Author.class);
Root<Author> root = criteria.from(Author.class);
criteria.select(root);
TypedQuery<Author> query = em.createQuery(criteria);
List<Author> list = query.getResultList();
```

The Criteria query is verbose but provides a lot more flexibility in constructing dynamic queries.

Native SQL

In certain cases, a native SQL statement may have to be used to query the database. The javax.persistence.EntityManager .createNativeQuery() method can used to specify the native SQL query string. Listing 2-6 shows how the `Author.findAll` named query can be executed as a native SQL query.

Listing 2-6   *Author Native Query*

```
em.createNativeQuery("select * from author", Author.class);
```

In this simplified case, the result set is mapped directly to the `Author` entity class. More complex mappings can be specified using the `@javax .persistence.SQLResultSetMapping` annotation.

NetBeans IDE provides wizards to query the database using native SQL query strings. Switch to the Services window (CTRL-3) and expand the Databases node. Right-click a table node, as shown in Figure 2-10, and choose View Data to view data in the related table in the database.

When the SQL editor opens, you have syntax coloring and code completion available to query the database and view the data directly in the IDE, as shown in Figure 2-11.

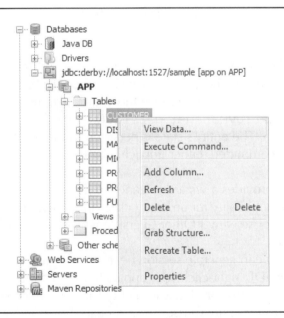

FIGURE 2-10.   *Viewing data defined in a database*

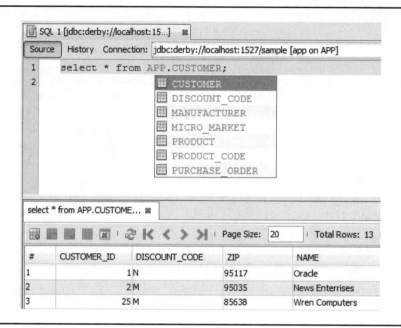

FIGURE 2-11. *Editing SQL query strings in the SQL editor*

A row from the database table can be removed by retrieving the required entity using any method. The `javax.persistence.EntityManager` `.remove()` method is called to remove the entity. Like the `javax` `.persistence.EntityManager.persist()` method, it must be called within a transaction. The entity's state is persisted to the database when the transaction is committed, either implicitly by the container or explicitly by the user.

NetBeans IDE provides a wizard to generate JPA controller classes that perform CRUD functionality for an entity class. In the IDE, right-click your application and choose New | Other | Persistence | JPA Controller Classes from Entity Classes.

In addition, you can generate session beans for the entity classes in the application. In the IDE, right-click your application and choose New | Other | Enterprise JavaBeans | Session Beans for Entity Classes, which displays the New Session Beans for Entity Classes wizard page shown in Figure 2-12.

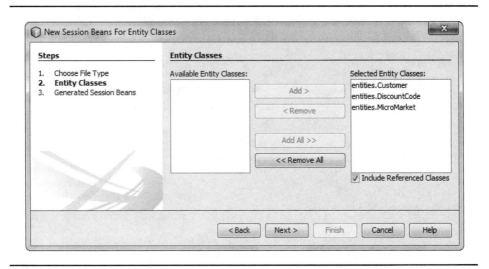

FIGURE 2-12. *Getting started creating session beans for existing entity classes*

Select any entity classes from the Available Entity Classes list in the left pane, and click the Add button. Any referenced entity classes are automatically added to the Selected Entity Class list in the right pane. If an entity class is grayed out, that indicates it is a referenced entity class.

Click Next to move to the Generated Session Beans page of the wizard, shown in Figure 2-13, and review or set the following:

- **Project** Displays the project where the entity classes will be saved. This field is read-only.

- **Location** Select the source folder where you want to create the entity class.

- **Package** Select an existing package from the Package drop-down list or type the name of a new package.

- **Create Interfaces** Select the session facade interfaces that you want the wizard to generate.

When you click Finish, the specified session beans are created, as shown in Figure 2-14.

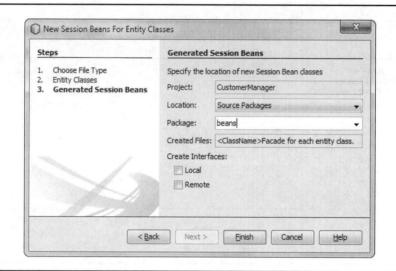

FIGURE 2-13. *Specifying details for creating session beans*

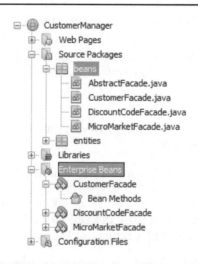

FIGURE 2-14. *New session beans created in the application*

Schema Generation

Typically, the database schema is already defined and JPA entity classes can be generated from that. Alternatively, entity managers can be configured to generate database table definitions in an existing schema or table generation scripts by specifying `javax.persistence.schema-generation.*` properties in `persistence.xml`.

Listing 2-7 shows how these properties can be configured on an entity manager.

Listing 2-7 *Generating Schema Using persistence.xml*

```
<persistence version="2.1" xmlns="http://xmlns.jcp.org/xml/ns/
persistence" xmlns:xsi="http://www.w3.org/2001/XMLSchema-instance"
xsi:schemaLocation="http://xmlns.jcp.org/xml/ns/persistence http://
xmlns.jcp.org/xml/ns/persistence/persistence_2_1.xsd">
    <persistence-unit name="authorPU" transaction-type="JTA">
        <properties>
            <property name="javax.persistence.schema-generation.
database.action" value="drop-and-create"/>
            <property name="javax.persistence.schema-generation.
create-source" value="script"/>
            <property name="javax.persistence.schema-generation.
drop-source" value="script"/>
            <property name="javax.persistence.schema-generation.
create-script-source" value="META-INF/create.sql"/>
            <property name="javax.persistence.schema-generation.
drop-script-source" value="META-INF/drop.sql"/>
            <property name="javax.persistence.sql-load-script-
source" value="META-INF/load.sql"/>
        </properties>
    </persistence-unit>
</persistence>
```

The following list explains these properties:

- The `javax.persistence.schema-generation.database
  .action` property value specifies to drop the existing tables and
  create them again. The possible values are `none`, `create`, `drop-
  and-create`, and `drop`.

- The `javax.persistence.schema-generation.create-source` property value specifies that the database creation should occur on the basis of the scripts.

- The `javax.persistence.schema-generation.drop-source` property value specifies that the database deletion should occur on the basis of the scripts.

  The possible values for the preceding two properties are `metadata`, `script`, `metadata-then-script`, and `script-then-metadata`. In this case, either script or metadata specified on the entity or a combination is used to create or drop tables.

- The `javax.persistence.schema-generation.create-script-source` property value specifies the location of the database creation script.

- The `javax.persistence.schema-generation.drop-script-source` property value specifies the location of the database deletion script.

- The `javax.persistence.sql-load-script-source` property value specifies the location of SQL bulk load script.

The last three property values specify that the script be packaged with the application. In this case, the location of the script is specified relative to the root of the persistence unit. Alternatively, a URL may externally identify the scripts.

These properties enable generation of the database schema from scripts or entity metadata. In addition to the properties described previously, the following properties may be used to specify the generation of scripts:

- `javax.persistence.schema-generation.scripts.action` can be used to specify which scripts need to be generated. The possible values are `none`, `create`, `drop-and-create`, and `drop`.

- `javax.persistence.schema-generation.scripts.create-target` and `javax.persistence.schema-generation.scripts.drop-target` can be used to specify the location of create and drop scripts. The locations are specified as strings corresponding to file URLs.

JPA provides several annotations such as `@javax.persistence`
`.Index`, `@javax.persistence.ForeignKey`, `@javax.persistence`
`.CollectionTable`, `@javax.persistence.JoinTable`, and `@javax`
`.persistence.JoinColumn` that can be specified on an entity to facilitate
database or scripts generation.

NetBeans IDE provides a wizard that simplifies the generation of scripts
based upon metadata. In the IDE, right-click your application and choose
New | Other | Persistence | DB Scripts for Entity Classes to generate the
scripts.

The Java Persistence API also provides a mechanism for second-level
caching, optimistic and pessimistic locking, entity lifecycle listeners, and many
more advanced concepts.

Summary

This chapter described the key concepts of persistence and explained how
data can be created, read, updated, and deleted from a relational database
using JPA. It also looked at how relational database tables can be easily
mapped to JPA entities, and it presented the requirements around their
packaging. Different types of Enterprise JavaBeans were introduced and their
transactional nature was explained briefly. Finally, this chapter demonstrated
how the database tables can be easily generated using the properties defined
in `persistence.xml`. NetBeans IDE tools and wizards were shown
throughout the chapter to highlight the simplified development process.
The next chapter will take these JPA entities and publish them as RESTful
endpoints.

CHAPTER
3

RESTful Resources

REST, or Representational State Transfer, is an architectural style for distributed systems such as the World Wide Web. This term was originally introduced and defined in 2000 by Roy Fielding in his dissertation *Architectural Styles and the Design of Network-based Software Architectures*. Fielding's motivation for choosing the dissertation topic was his "desire to understand and evaluate the architectural design of network-based application software through principled use of architectural constraints, thereby obtaining the functional, performance, and social properties desired of an architecture." See www.ics.uci.edu/~fielding/pubs/dissertation/introduction.htm. This was achieved by defining a framework to understand the software architecture of network-based applications. The thesis then describes how REST is used to guide the design and development of the architecture for the modern Web.

Modern applications typically publish their APIs using REST architecture. For example, Twitter's REST API is published at https://dev.twitter.com/docs/api. Integrating any Twitter functionality, such as searching for tweets with a particular hashtag or obtaining a collection of the most recent tweets, can be accomplished by invoking the Twitter REST API and processing the result in your application.

This chapter explains the key REST principles and how REST services can be published and invoked from Java.

REST Principles

The World Wide Web is the largest implementation of a system conforming to the REST architectural style. In that context, REST is a set of principles that defines how web standards, such as HTTP and URIs, are supposed to be used for building your applications. To successfully build Java EE applications that utilize web standards, you'll need to understand the guiding principles of REST architecture. These principles will guide you as you define resources and set up services.

The guiding principles of REST architecture are

- **Resource** The key information in this architecture is a *resource*. Any information that can be named can be a resource: a document or image, a book, an author, a collection of other resources, and so on.

- **Client and server** A client-server model is used where a client initiates a request to the server; the server processes the request and returns an appropriate response to the client. Requests and responses are built around the transfer of resources.

- **Identification of resources** Every resource can be uniquely identified on the client and server. Everything on the Web can be identified as a resource, and each resource can be uniquely identified by a URI.

- **Resources are available in multiple representations** A resource can be represented in multiple formats, defined by a media type. The client and server can negotiate on the content type of the resource.

- **Standard methods can be used to manipulate these resources** Each resource can be created, read, updated, and deleted using standard methods. HTTP defines *verbs* such as GET, PUT, POST, and DELETE to manipulate resources on the Web.

- **Communicate statelessly** The server does not retain any communication state for any of the clients beyond a single request. If state is required, then it should be kept on the client or converted into resource state. This allows the server to scale much better.

You will see how each of these principles is used with the Java API for REST as you continue in this chapter, and with the JavaScript API for REST in Chapter 5.

Java API for RESTful Web Services

Java API for RESTful Web Services (JAX-RS) defines a standard, annotation-driven API that helps developers develop and invoke a RESTful web service in Java. JAX-RS 1.1 was first included in the Java EE 6 platform. Java EE 7 includes JAX-RS 2.0, which is a deep revision of JAX-RS that adds several features that can handle the most modern style of web applications.

Let's consider a REST resource that provides create, read, update, and delete operations on an author database. Such a REST resource can be invoked using any of the standard HTTP verbs such as POST, GET, PUT, or DELETE. The endpoint should have the capability to publish and consume resource representations in multiple formats. A complete list of authors or a specific author should be accessible. A REST endpoint that publishes and consumes multiple representations of the author resource using common HTTP verbs is shown in Listing 3-1.

Listing 3-1 *Author REST Resource*

```java
@Path("authors")
public class AuthorResource {
  @Inject AuthorSessionBean bean;

  @GET
  @Produces({"application/xml;qs=0.75","application/json;qs=1"})
    public List<Author> findAll() {
    return bean.findAllAuthors();
  }

  @GET
  @Path("{id}")
  @Produces({"application/xml;qs=0.75","application/json;qs=1"})
  public Author find(@PathParam("id") Integer id) {
    return bean.findAuthor(id);
  }

  @GET
  @Path("count")
  @Produces("text/plain")
  public int count() {
    return bean.countAuthors();
  }

  @POST
  @Consumes({"application/xml", "application/json"})
  public void create(Author author) {
    bean.createAuthor(author);
  }

  @PUT
  @Consumes({"application/xml", "application/json"})
  public void edit(Author author) {
    bean.updateAuthor(author);
  }

  @DELETE
  @Path("{id}")
  public void remove(@PathParam("id") Integer id) {
    bean.removeAuthor(id);
  }
}
```

The following information will help you to understand this code:

- A POJO can be converted to a REST resource by adding `@javax .ws.rs.Path` annotation to the class. The annotation defines the URI where the resource is accessible—`authors` in this case. Paths are relative. For an annotated class, the base URI is defined using `@javax.ws.rs.ApplicationPath` annotation on a class that extends the `javax.ws.rs.core.Application` class. The complete URI of the resource is defined as:

  ```
  http://<host>:<port>/<webapp-context-root>/<base-URI>/<resource-URI>
  ```

  So if the resource is packaged in a WAR file with the context root "sahara" and deployed on the host "localhost" and the port "8080" with the base URI "webresources," then the complete path of the resource would be

  ```
  http://localhost:8080/sahara/webresources/authors
  ```

- A subresource of the main resource can be defined by annotating a method of the root resource with `@javax.ws.rs.Path` annotation. The base URI of this subresource is the effective URI of the containing class. The annotated method is invoked whenever the resource is accessed using the complete path defined by the base URI and the path specified on the method. In Listing 3-1, the `count()` method is called if the resource is accessed at the `webresources/authors/count` path. Note that the `count()` method is also annotated with `@javax.ws.rs.GET` annotation, but it is available at a different path because it is defined as a subresource.

  The `@javax.ws.rs.Path` annotation can take a URI template parameter. The value passed to this template parameter can be bound to a resource method parameter using `@javax.ws.rs.PathParam` annotation. In Listing 3-1, the `find()` method is called if the resource is accessed at the `webresources/authors/`*nnn* path, where *nnn* is some value. The `id()` method parameter is populated with the value *nnn* and invokes the `find()` method on the EJB.

- In addition, although not shown in Listing 3-1, cookies can be bound to a parameter using `@javax.ws.rs.CookieParam` annotation, HTTP headers can be bound to a parameter using `@javax.ws.rs .HeaderParam` annotation, a matrix parameter can be bound to a method parameter using @javax.ws.rs.MatrixParam annotation, and parameters coming through an HTML form can be bound to a method parameter using @javax.ws.rs.FormParam annotation.

■ Validation constraints, although not shown in Listing 3-1, can be specified on the method parameters to ensure that only valid values are accepted for method parameters. A javax.constraint .ConstraintViolation exception is thrown if the incoming values do not meet the criteria (for example, an alphabetic value is sent when only a numeric value is expected). This can be easily specified using any of the @javax.validation.constraints .Min, @javax.validation.constraints.Max, @javax .validation.constraints.Digits, or similar annotations on the method parameter. The specification even defines an extensible mechanism by which custom constraints meeting application needs can be easily defined.

■ Any Java EE component can be injected into the resource using Dependency Injection. An Enterprise JavaBean, AuthorSessionBean, is injected in Listing 3-1 to ensure that all the business logic is defined in the bean. This ensures that any code related to retrieving, adding, or updating from the database is automatically done within a transaction and stays within the EJB. This is important as the runtime container starts and commits or rolls back the transaction to ensure the ACID properties of the underlying database are preserved automatically. Otherwise, the application will have to manually create a transaction and manage it by itself.

■ Java EE 7 introduces @javax.transaction.Transactional annotation, although not shown in Listing 3-1, allows all methods within a bean or any method in the bean to be selectively transactional. This is implemented as a CDI interceptor binding and allows the application developer a choice of using EJB or a POJO for container-managed transactions.

■ Different HTTP verbs such as GET, PUT, POST, and DELETE are identified by the corresponding annotations in the javax.ws.rs package.

■   The `findAll()` method is called when the resource is accessed
using HTTP GET. The path of the resource or subresource is defined
as explained earlier. The media type generated by a method is
described using `@javax.ws.rs.Produces` annotation. A method
can support one or more media types, and the client requesting the
resource can ask for a specific media type using the standard HTTP
`Accept` header. The return value from the method is converted to
the appropriate media type and sent on the wire to the client. If this
annotation is not specified, then the container assumes that any type
can be produced. It is recommended to specify the return media type
to ensure that the client and endpoint are aware of the contract.

■   JAX-RS provides the `javax.ws.rs.core.MediaType` class,
which provides strongly typed fields for commonly used media
types. For example, `MediaType.APPLICATION_JSON_TYPE`
can be used instead of `application/json`. However, some
developers prefer the literal to be specified in their endpoint because
it improves the readability of the code.

■   If a resource is represented using multiple media types and the client
has not indicated any preference, then the endpoint can indicate a
media preference using the qs attribute (short for "quality of service").
qs is a floating-point number with a value in the range of 0.000
through 1.000 and indicates the relative quality of a representation
compared to the others available, independent of the client's
capabilities. A representation with a qs value of 0.000 will never
be chosen. A representation with no qs parameter value is given
a qs factor of 1.0. In Listing 3-1, if a client requests the resource
with the `*/*` media type or no preferred representation, then JSON
representation of the resource is returned because that has a higher
priority (`qs=1`) than the only other media type listed, XML (`qs=0.75`).
However, if the client explicitly asks for the `application/xml`
media type, then an XML representation is returned instead.

■   By default, standard media types such as `application/xml` and
`application/json` are supported. Providing entity providers that
know how to read/write media types from the stream can support
application-specific media types.

■   The `@javax.ws.rs.Consumes` annotation is used to define
the media type that can be consumed by a method. A method

can consume multiple media types, and the actual media type is identified using the HTTP `Content-Type` header. If this annotation is not specified, then the container assumes that any type can be consumed.

■ A resource can be updated by annotating a method with `@javax .ws.rs.PUT` annotation. Similarly, a resource can be deleted by annotating a method with `@javax.ws.rs.DELETE` annotation.

Out of the box, NetBeans IDE provides many wizards to help you get started developing web services, many of which are shown in Figure 3-1.

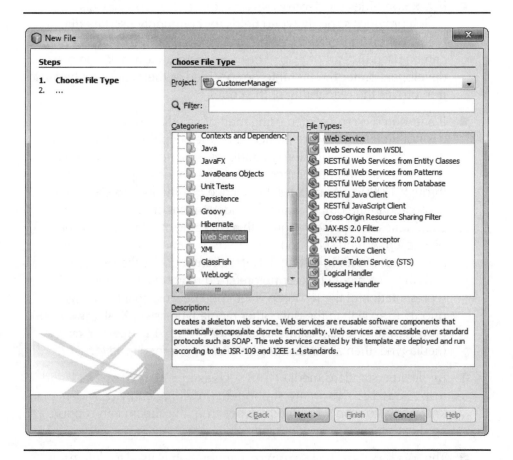

FIGURE 3-1. *New File dialog showing web service wizards*

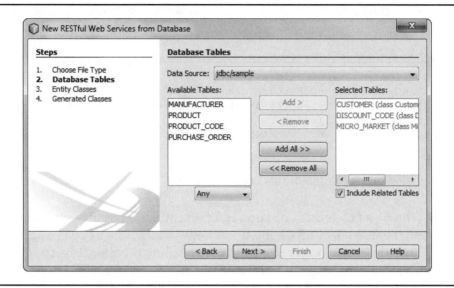

FIGURE 3-2.   *RESTful Web Services from Database*

For example, RESTful web services can be generated directly from your database. Figure 3-2 shows one step in this process. No entity classes need be present in your application because the wizard will create those from your database, too.

JAX-RS Client API

Prior to the release of JAX-RS 2.0, invoking a REST resource required writing boilerplate code using `java.net.URL` and a related set of classes. Marshaling and unmarshaling Java objects to resource representations had to be done manually. Any errors received from the endpoint had to be again manually mapped to more meaningful exceptions on the client side. JAX-RS 2.0 introduces a Client API that can be used to invoke a REST resource from a Java application. This API can be used to consume any web service exposed on top of an HTTP protocol or its extension (e.g., WebDAV) and is not restricted to services implemented using JAX-RS.

Let's see how a REST endpoint can be invoked using this API (Listing 3-2).

Listing 3-2 *JAX-RS Client API Usage*

```
Client client = ClientBuilder.newClient();
client.register(JacksonFeature.class);
WebTarget target = client.target(http://localhost:8080/sahara/
webresources/authors);
Author[] authors = target.request("application/json").get(Author[].
class);
```

The following list explains this code:

- The `javax.ws.rs.client.ClientBuilder` is the entry point to the fluent JAX-RS Client API. A new `javax.ws.rs.client .Client` instance can be created by calling the `newClient()` method. This instance is then used to build and execute client requests in order to consume responses returned. It is recommended to create only a required number of `Client` instances in the application, as the initialization and disposal of a `Client` instance may be a rather expensive operation.

- The web resource URI is passed to the `target()` method and builds a `javax.ws.rs.client.WebTarget` instance. A builder-style API is used to build a request to the targeted web resource. The `request()` method starts building the request. Optionally, the media types acceptable in the response can be specified as a method parameter. These types can also be specified as parameters to `request().accept()` method. Once the request is prepared, it can be invoked using the intuitive `get()`, `put()`, `post()`, and `delete()` methods. The response can be automatically converted to a Java type by specifying the type as a method parameter. In this case, the response is returned as an array of `Author`.

Out of the box, NetBeans IDE provides a New RESTful Java Client wizard to let you quickly and easily create a Java web service client for an existing RESTful web service. Figure 3-3 shows the final step in this wizard.

After you select the location of the web service and click Finish, the IDE will create the Java client for you. Alternatively, you can create an

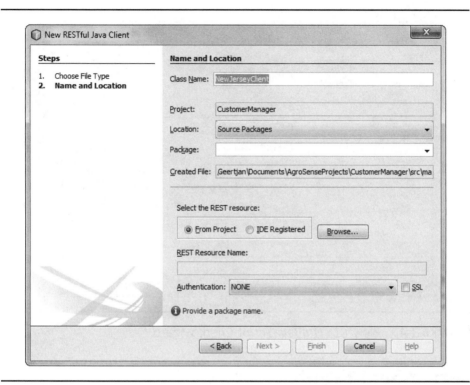

FIGURE 3-3.   *New RESTful Java Client wizard*

HTML/JavaScript/CSS front end for your RESTful web service via the RESTful JavaScript Client wizard, as shown in Figure 3-4.

In a standard HTTP request-response scenario, a JavaScript client or a Java client using the JAX-RS Client API opens a connection to the resource endpoint, sends an HTTP request to the server (for example, an HTTP GET request), and then receives an HTTP response back; the server closes the connection once the response is fully sent/received. The client *always* initiates the request and "pulls" the information from the server as required. Sometimes there may be a need for a server to asynchronously "push" information to the client. For example, a stock ticker endpoint can push the updated stock price to the client. In our example, information about a new book can be pushed to the client.

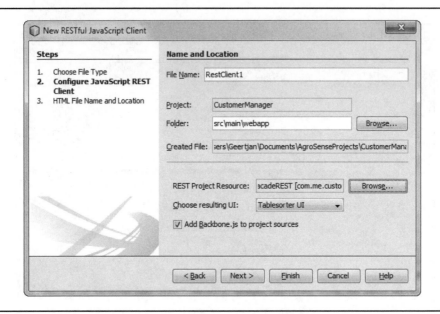

FIGURE 3-4. *New RESTful JavaScript Client wizard*

Server-Sent Events

Typically, a client initiates a request to the server and receives a response. *Server-Sent Events (SSE)* is a mechanism that allows the server to asynchronously push the data from the server to the client whenever a new "chunk" of data is available. The client is still responsible for establishing the connection with the server. When new data is ready to be sent on the server, the server sends the data event to the client, hence the name, Server-Sent Events.

A server-sent event is generated on the server side with a predefined media type of `text/event-stream`. There is no restriction for a media type used in individual event messages. On the client side, the standard *EventSource* JavaScript API is used to open an HTTP connection for receiving push notifications from the server. These events are received in callback handlers registered in the client JavaScript and are used to update the client.

Note that SSE will be a final specification along with the rest of HTML5. This is targeted to be final in late 2014. Until then, SSE cannot be added as a standard API to JAX-RS. However, the JAX-RS reference implementation, Jersey, has added support for SSE. This chapter will use Jersey to implement that functionality in our application and explain SSE.

Let's say you have a `Book` resource to represent the books written by an author. This resource can be described following the design pattern used for the `Author` resource. Now let's say you update the `Book` resource endpoint such that it generates a server-sent event whenever a new book is added.

First of all, you need to enable support for SSE for the JAX-RS application. As this is not part of the standard JAX-RS API, you need to update the `pom.xml` file to include the SSE *media type module,* as shown in Listing 3-3.

Listing 3-3 *Jersey SSE Media Dependency*

```
<dependency>
    <groupId>org.glassfish.jersey.media</groupId>
    <artifactId>jersey-media-sse</artifactId>
    <version>2.0</version>
    <scope>provided</scope>
</dependency>
```

Next, you need to register `org.glassfish.jersey.media.sse` `.SseFeature` in the `Application` class, as shown in Listing 3-4.

Listing 3-4 *Adding SseFeature to JAX-RS*

```
public Set<Class<?>> getClasses() {
  Set<Class<?>> resources = new java.util.HashSet<>();

  // . . .
  resources.add(SseFeature.class);
  return resources;
}
```

The `getClasses()` method returns a set of root resources, feature, and feature classes. Adding `SseFeature`, in addition to other resources, to the set of classes returned from this method takes care of registering the feature.

Then, you need to add or update methods that push SSE to the client, as shown in Listing 3-5.

Listing 3-5 *Updating SSE Methods*

```
@Path("books")
public class BooksResource {
    //. . .
    private final SseBroadcaster BROADCASTER = new
SseBroadcaster();
```

```
@POST
@Override
@Consumes({"application/xml", "application/json"})
public void create(Books book) {
    bean.createBooks(book);

    OutboundEvent event = new OutboundEvent.Builder()
            .data(String.class, "New book \""
                + book.getTitle()
                + "\" with ISBN \""
                + book.getIsbn()
                + "\" added")
            .build();
    BROADCASTER.broadcast(event);
}

@GET
@Path("events")
@Produces(SseFeature.SERVER_SENT_EVENTS)
public EventOutput getEvents() {
    final EventOutput eventOutput = new EventOutput();
    this.BROADCASTER.add(eventOutput);
    return eventOutput;
}

//. . .
}
```

Listing 3-5 shows only the updated methods. The following list explains this code:

■ Generating SSE on the server side is a two-step process. First, clients that want to listen to SSE send a GET request to this resource at /books/events, which is handled by the getEvents() method. Second, the method creates a new EventOutput instance representing a connection to the requesting client and registers it with the broadcaster using the add(eventOutput) method. EventOutput allows the underlying connection to remain open so that the application can push SSE later.

- @Produces on this method ensures that the media type of the returned type is text/event-stream.

- SseBroadcaster provides a convenient way of grouping multiple EventOutput instances and broadcasting new events to all the client connections grouped in the broadcaster.

- SseFeature adds support for a new entity Java type, namely OutboundEvent. This entity can be used to create any server outbound events. SseFeature also adds support for InboundEvent, which can be used for inbound client events for the JAX-RS Client API.

- The create() method is updated to broadcast a message to all the clients listening on their SSE connections. A new SSE outbound event is built in the standard way and passed to the broadcaster by calling the broadcast message. The broadcaster internally invokes write(OutboundEvent) on all registered EventOutput instances. As mentioned earlier, there is no restriction on the media type for individual event messages. This application is sending a plain text message as a server-sent event.

- Individual EventOutput instances can be stored in a collection and iterated over in the create() method. However, SseBroadcaster also internally identifies and handles client disconnects. When a client closes the connection, the broadcaster detects this and removes the stale connection from the internal collection of the registered EventOutput instances. The broadcaster also frees all the server-side resources associated with the stale connection. Additionally, SseBroadcaster is implemented to be thread-safe so that clients can connect and disconnect at any time; SseBroadcaster will always broadcast messages only to the most recent collection of registered and active set of clients.

In addition to addressing many other HTML5 client-specific topics, Chapter 5 will show you how SSE is consumed on the client side.

Summary

You started this chapter by learning about the origins of REST and what the guiding principles are for a RESTful architecture. You then learned from the Java EE perspective how a RESTful resource can be developed, deployed, and invoked using the standard Java API for RESTful Web Services (JAX-RS). Design patterns for integrating other Java EE technologies with your RESTful resources were discussed. Finally, you were introduced to how support for Server-Sent Events can be easily incorporated using the JAX-RS reference implementation, Jersey. You were also shown throughout the chapter how NetBeans IDE can speed the creation and implementation of these Java EE features. In the next chapter, you will be shown how to work with an exciting new area of HTML5 called WebSocket.

CHAPTER
4

WebSocket

H TTP was designed to share information over the Internet, and it has served very well in that respect. But it is inherently half-duplex; that is, the client (in most cases the browser) initiates a request to an HTTP server, and the server processes the request and responds to the client. Web applications that require the server to push information to the client have typically achieved that functionality by abusing the protocol, such as via polling and long polling.

In polling, a client requests a resource from a server using normal HTTP at regular intervals. A new connection to the server is opened at the specified interval, say after three seconds, and the server returns any new information in the response. The connection is closed after the client has received the information. It is likely that new information is not available for each request. This also requires tuning the interval at which the information is requested, and is generally application-specific. Therefore, this is not a very efficient way to push information from server to client.

In long polling, a client requests a resource from a server using normal HTTP. The server does not immediately respond with the requested information but rather waits and responds when new information is available. The client receives the new information, closes the connection, and immediately sends another request to the server. This type of polling keeps an open connection between the client and the server indefinitely, with possibly no data exchanged during the majority of the time. It also requires opening a new connection after a response is received. This is also not efficient utilization of resources.

The Server-Sent Events (SSE) specification included in HTML5 provides a similar mechanism to the long polling mechanism, except it does not send only one message per connection. The client sends a request and the server holds open a connection until a new message is ready. It sends a message back to the client when new information is available while still keeping the connection open. This allows the connection to be reused for subsequent messages, or events.

For a regular HTTP request and response, each HTTP request requires establishing a new TCP connection to the server, and that connection is terminated after the HTTP response has been received. Setting up a TCP connection is an expensive operation but is rather invisible if the number of HTTP requests is low. If the number of requests increases, then creation and termination of the TCP connection with each HTTP message exchange reduces the overall performance of the application.

HTTP also has a high overhead for a wire protocol. A minimum set of headers must be exchanged on-the-wire between the client and the server in order to fulfill the protocol requirements. There is a processing cost associated with parsing these headers that further reduces the performance of an application if the number of message exchanges increases.

In short, HTTP is a half-duplex and verbose protocol that is inefficient for full-duplex and bidirectional communication between client and server. This is exactly the need served by WebSocket.

What Is WebSocket?

WebSocket is a full-duplex, bidirectional protocol that uses a single TCP connection for exchanging messages in both directions.

WebSocket is defined by two different specifications:

- **WebSocket Protocol, RFC 6455**　http://tools.ietf.org/html/rfc6455

- **W3C WebSocket API**　www.w3.org/TR/websockets/

RFC 6455 defines how a WebSocket connection can be established using a *handshake*. It also defines the wire protocol for WebSocket message exchange. The W3C WebSocket API is a JavaScript API that is implemented by different browsers. This API can then be used by web applications to make connections to WebSocket endpoints and exchange messages.

WebSocket Handshake

Section 14.42 of HTTP 1.1 (RFC 2616) defines an upgrade mechanism that allows a transition from the HTTP 1.1 protocol to a different protocol. In this case, to the WebSocket protocol. After an upgrade is negotiated between the client and the server, the subsequent requests use the newly chosen protocol for message exchanges.

RFC 6455 defines how a WebSocket client can make an HTTP upgrade request. This is called a WebSocket client handshake and is shown in Listing 4-1.

Listing 4-1   *WebSocket Client Handshake*

```
GET /chat HTTP/1.1
Host: server.example.com
Upgrade: websocket
Connection: Upgrade
Sec-WebSocket-Key: dGhlIHNhbXBsZSBub25jZQ==
Origin: http://example.com
Sec-WebSocket-Protocol: chat
Sec-WebSocket-Version: 13
```

Listing 4-1 shows a typical client opening handshake request. The header fields in the handshake may be sent in any order. In this fragment, the first couple of lines are like a usual HTTP request, indicating that this is a GET request and identifying the host and URI to which the request is addressed. The key part to notice here is that the WebSocket protocol attempts to achieve bidirectional communication in the context of existing HTTP infrastructure. This allows the protocol to work over HTTP ports 80 and 443 and to support HTTP proxies and intermediaries.

The WebSocket-related header fields in Listing 4-1 are as follows:

- The `Upgrade` and `Connection` header fields mark this HTTP request as an upgrade request, specifically requesting an upgrade to WebSocket.

- Different subprotocols can be negotiated using the `Sec-WebSocket-Protocol` header field. If you choose to define a subprotocol, that same field must be included on both the server and client. It is also recommended that any subprotocol be registered with the Internet Assigned Numbers Authority (IANA) to help avoid naming conflicts.

- The `Sec-WebSocket-Version` header is returned by the server and must be set to a value of 13.

- The `Origin` header field is used to protect against unauthorized cross-origin use of the WebSocket server by scripts using the WebSocket API in a web browser.

- If the server is capable of handling this upgrade request, then it processes the received `Sec-WebSocket-Key` header field using a predefined algorithm and returns the generated value in the server handshake response.

A typical server opening handshake response looks like this:

```
HTTP/1.1 101 Switching Protocols
Upgrade: websocket
Connection: Upgrade
Sec-WebSocket-Accept: s3pPLMBiTxaQ9kYGzzhZRbK+xOo=
```

The first line is an HTTP status line and indicates that the handshake was successful. The `Upgrade` and `Connection` header fields complete the HTTP upgrade. The `Sec-WebSocket-Accept` header field must contain the value generated on the server using the predefined algorithm defined by RFC 6455. All these header fields must be present in order for the handshake to be complete.

Once a connection is established between the client and server, they are considered to be peers with equal capabilities. Each can send messages to the other without waiting for the other to respond.

Either peer can initiate the closing handshake by sending a Close control frame with data containing a specified control sequence. The receiving peer sends a Close control frame in response indicating that the connection is now closed.

A peer does not send any further data after sending a Close control frame. Similarly, a peer discards any further data received after receiving a Close control frame. The WebSocket closing handshake then initiates the TCP closing handshake as well.

WebSocket API

The WebSocket API (www.w3.org/TR/websockets/) enables web pages to use the WebSocket protocol for two-way communication with a remote host.

WebSocket can send and receive text and binary data. The API provides an overloaded `send` method that can send text or binary data by taking any of the following parameters:

- Text: `String`

- Binary: `Blob, ArrayBuffer, ArrayBufferView`

The API provides event handlers that are invoked for different lifecycle events and when a message is received:

- Lifecycle events: `onopen(), onerror(), onclose()`

- Message: `onmessage()`

Java API for WebSocket

Java API for WebSocket defines a set of Java APIs for the development of WebSocket applications. The API enables you to define a server endpoint and a client endpoint. A server endpoint listens for requests from multiple clients. A client endpoint communicates with only one server.

You can define a server endpoint or a client endpoint by decorating a POJO with annotations from the Java API for WebSocket. Such an endpoint is called an *annotated endpoint*. Alternatively, you can extend some of the classes from the Java API for WebSocket to provide a more fine-grained control over the endpoint. This type of endpoint is called a *programmatic endpoint*.

In this chapter, we'll build the legendary game of tic-tac-toe using WebSocket. In this game, two players, identified by X and O, take turns marking the squares in a nine-square grid composed of three columns and three rows. The player who succeeds in placing their respective mark (X or O) in three consecutive squares horizontally, vertically, or diagonally wins the game.

The annotated endpoint for the game is shown in Listing 4-2.

Listing 4-2 *WebSocket Endpoint Annotations*

```
@ServerEndpoint(value = "/endpoint",
        decoders = BoardDecoder.class)
public class TicTactToeEndpoint {

    private static final Map<String, String> games = new
HashMap<>();

    @OnOpen
    public void onOpen(Session session) throws IOException {
        if (games.isEmpty()) {
            games.put(session.getId(), "x");
            session.getBasicRemote().sendText("You play X");
        } else {
            games.put(session.getId(), "y");
            session.getBasicRemote().sendText("You play O");
        }
    }

    @OnMessage
    public void onMessage(Board board, Session session) throws
IOException, EncodeException {
        if (board.getStatus() != null && board.getStatus().
equals("clear")) {
```

```
        for (Session s : session.getOpenSessions()) {
            games.remove(s.getId());
            s.close();
        }
        return;
    }

    String symbol = null;
    for (String game : games.keySet()) {
        if (game.equals(session.getId())) {
            symbol = games.get(game);
            break;
        }
    }

    // Create JSON structure
    StringWriter writer = new StringWriter();
    JsonGenerator gen = Json.createGenerator(writer);
    gen.writeStartObject();
    gen.write("symbol", symbol);
    gen.write("x", board.getX() + "");
    gen.write("y", board.getY() + "");
    gen.writeEnd();
    gen.flush();

    // Send to all other open clients
    for (Session s : session.getOpenSessions()) {
        if (!s.equals(session)) {
            s.getBasicRemote().sendText(writer.toString());
        }
    }
  }
}
}
```

The following list explains the code shown in Listing 4-2:

■ `@ServerEndpoint` is a class-level annotation that decorates
    a POJO to be a WebSocket endpoint. The annotation allows the
    developer to define the URL where this endpoint is published using
    the `value` attribute.

    By default, a new instance of the endpoint is created per application
    per virtual machine (VM) to represent the logical endpoint per
    connected peer. Each instance of the endpoint in this typical case
    handles connections to the endpoint from one and only one peer.

- The `configurator` attribute can be used to specify a `ServerEndpointConfig.Configurator` class that can be used to provide a singleton instance of the endpoint for all the peers. Custom configuration algorithms, such as intercepting the opening handshake, can also be specified using this configurator. This attribute is not used in this example.

  Additional configuration information can be specified using other attributes; for example, the `decoders` attribute defines an ordered array of decoder classes used by this endpoint. `BoardDecoder` `.class` converts WebSocket messages into an application-defined `Board` object. The implementation creates a new instance of the decoder per endpoint instance per connection.

- The annotated class must have a public no-args constructor.

- `games` is a Map object that stores the unique identifier of the client with the corresponding symbol.

- `@OnOpen` is a method-level annotation that decorates a Java method to be called when a new WebSocket connection is open. The method may take the following parameters:

  - An optional `Session` parameter that represents a conversation between two WebSocket endpoints

  - An optional `EndpointConfig` parameter that contains the information used during the handshake for this endpoint

  - Zero to *n* String parameters annotated with `@PathParam` annotation that maps the URI template specified in the path mapping of the endpoint

  This method defines the player's symbol, puts it in the `games` Map object keyed by the client identifier, and also sends a message back to the player indicating the symbol.

- `@OnMessage` is a method-level annotation that decorates a Java method to be called when an incoming WebSocket message is received. Each WebSocket endpoint may have only one method for each of the native WebSocket message formats: text, binary, and pong.

If the method is handling text messages, then the parameter may be one of the following:

- `String` to receive the whole message

- Java primitive or class equivalent to receive the whole message converted to that type

- `String` and `boolean` pair to receive the message in parts

- `Reader` to receive the whole message as a blocking stream

- Any object parameter for which the endpoint is a text decoder

If the method is handling binary messages, then the parameter may be one of the following:

- `byte[]` or `ByteBuffer` to receive the whole message

- `byte[]` and `boolean` pair, or `ByteBuffer` and `boolean` pair, to receive the message in parts

- `InputStream` to receive the whole message as a blocking stream

- Any object parameter for which the endpoint is a binary decoder

If the method is handling pong messages, then the parameter should be `PongMessage`.

In this case, `Board` is decoded by `BoardDecoder`. An optional `Session` parameter is specified to represent the conversation between two endpoints.

If the received board status is set to `"clear"`, then all games are removed from the games Map and the connection to the client peer is also closed. Otherwise, the symbol is retrieved from the games Map.

- Java API for JSON Processing provides a standard API to parse and generate JSON. It allows production/consumption of JSON text in a streaming fashion (similar to StAX API for XML), or allows the building of a Java object model (similar to DOM API for XML).

  A streaming generator is created using the `Json.createGenerator()` method. A `Writer` or an `OutputStream` can be passed to this method. A `Writer` is used to write to a character stream, and an `OutputStream` is used to write to a byte stream. A JSON structure indicating the current symbol used in the game and the x and y coordinates in the grid are created. It looks like:

```
{
    "symbol": "x",
    "x": "1",
    "y": "2"
}
```

■ The `session.getOpenSessions()` method provides a list of all the listening clients. This generated JSON text is sent to all the listening clients, which then update the state of the game board.

`BoardDecoder.class` decodes the incoming text payload and converts it to the application-specific `Board` class. Listing 4-3 shows what it looks like.

Listing 4-3 *BoardDecoder Class*

```
public class BoardDecoder implements Decoder.Text<Board> {
    @Override
    public Board decode(String string) throws DecodeException {
        System.out.println("BoardDecoder.decoding: " + string);
        JsonObject jsonObject = Json.createReader(new
StringReader(string)).readObject();
        Board board = new Board();
        if (jsonObject.getString("x") != null) {
            board.setX(Integer.parseInt(jsonObject.
getString("x")));
        }
        if (jsonObject.getString("y") != null) {
            board.setY(Integer.parseInt(jsonObject.
getString("y")));
        }
        if (jsonObject.getString("status", null) != null) {
            board.setStatus((jsonObject.getString("status")));
        }

        System.out.println("decoded: " + board);
        return board;
    }

    @Override
    public boolean willDecode(String string) {
        try {
            Json.createReader(new StringReader(string)).
```

```
readObject();
            return true;
        } catch (JsonException ex) {
            ex.printStackTrace();
            return false;
        }
    }

    @Override
    public void init(EndpointConfig ec) {
        System.out.println("BoardDecoder.init");
    }

    @Override
    public void destroy() {
        System.out.println("BoardDecoder.destroy");
    }
}
```

The following list describes the code shown in Listing 4-3:

- The text-based decoder typically implements the `Decoder.Text<T>` interface, and the binary-based decoder typically implements the `Decoder.Binary<T>` interface.

  In addition, there are `Decoder.TextStream` and `Decoder.BinaryStream` interfaces that read the WebSocket message from a character or binary stream, respectively.

- The `Decoder.Text<T>` interface requires implementing the `decode()` method that decodes the given String into an object of type `T`. In our method implementation, the message payload is read using a `Reader` and then converted into a `JsonObject`. Different values read from the parsed object are used to populate the application-specific `Board` class. An overloaded version of the `getString()` method is used to define a default value of `null`.

- The interface also requires implementing the `willDecode()` method. This method returns `true` if the given String can be decoded to an object of type `T`. Our method implementation tries to parse the message payload as `JsonObject`. If the parsing is successful, then it returns `true`; it returns `false` otherwise.

Other lifecycle methods like `init()` and `destroy()` need to be implemented. They are no-op in this case.

HTML5 Client Application for WebSocket

The client-side code for the tic-tac-toe application that you've been working on so far is all located in the Web Pages folder in the NetBeans IDE navigator window, as shown in Figure 4-1. Over the next sections of this chapter, you will build the client code that connects to the WebSocket service you created in previous sections.

HTML5 Application Setup

The client side of this tic-tac-toe application is created using a couple of different JavaScript frameworks. Twitter Bootstrap is used for the basic look and feel, as well as to enable the application to resize as the browser window changes size—called *responsive design* (covered in more detail in Chapter 5). The second framework is Knockout.js.

Listing 4-4 shows how the `index.html` file is set up to load all of the dependencies.

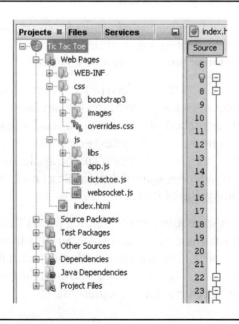

FIGURE 4-1. *Client code in IDE*

Listing 4-4 *Loading Dependencies in index.html*

```
<head>
    <title>Tic-Tac-Toe</title>
    <meta charset="UTF-8">
    <meta name="viewport" content="width=device-width">
    <link rel="stylesheet" href="css/bootstrap3/bootstrap.css"/>
    <link rel="stylesheet" href="css/overrides.css"/>
    <script type="text/javascript" src="js/libs/jquery/jquery.
js"></script>
    <script type="text/javascript" src="js/libs/knockout/knockout-
min.js"></script>
    <script type="text/javascript" src="js/libs/bootstrap3/
bootstrap.js"></script>
    <script type="text/javascript" src="js/websocket.js"></script>
    <script type="text/javascript" src="js/tictactoe.js"></script>
    <script type="text/javascript" src="js/app.js"></script>
</head>
```

Let's take a look at how the application is configured in the <head> section of the index.html file. This application uses Knockout.js (http://knockoutjs .com/) to implement a Model-View-ViewModel (MVVM) architectural pattern. All of this will be explained in much more detail in Chapter 5, but for now, you can see in this code that the Knockout JavaScript libraries are being added with a simple <script> reference. The other JavaScript libraries being used are jQuery and Bootstrap.

To get the proper layout and style for the game, Twitter Bootstrap CSS files and an override CSS file are referenced. CSS files are read in the order in which they are listed, so the override.css files must come last in the list of all CSS files.

The two JavaScript files that you will work with the most for connecting up the WebSocket interface and managing the game itself are found in websocket.js and tictactoe.js.

Listing 4-5 shows the main sections of the body of the index.html file and how the view layer of the application is set up.

Listing 4-5 *Main Sections of index.html File*

```
<header class="header">
    <div >
      <div id="title" class="headertext text-center">Tic-Tac-Toe</
div>
    </div>
</header>
```

```
<section id="playerInfo" class="col-sm-3">
    <div class="row">
        <div id="playerName" data-bind="text: playerName">Player
One</div>
        <div id="playStatus" class="playerStatus" data-
bind="visible: showStatus, text: gameStatus">You Go First!</div>
        <!--<div id="playSecond" class="playerStatus" data-
bind="visible: gameOver">You Win!!</div>-->
        <div id="win-lose" class="win-lose" data-bind="visible:
gameOver">You Win!!</div>
        <div id="output"></div>
    </div>
    <div class="row">
        <div class="btn" data-bind="click: clearBoard">New
Game?</div>
    </div>
</section>

<section id="boardLayout" class="col-sm-9">
    <div id="board" class="container col-xs-12">
        <div id="row1" class="row col-xs-12">
            <div id="1" class="col-sm-offset-4 col-xs-1 game-
cell"><img id="cellImage1-1" data-x="1" data-y="1" class="blank"
src="css/images/blank.png" data-bind="click: gameCellClicked"/></
div>
            <div id="2" class="col-xs-1 game-cell"><img
id="cellImage1-2" class="blank" data-x="1" data-y="2" src="css/
images/blank.png" data-bind="click: gameCellClicked"/></div>
            <div id="3" class="col-xs-1 game-cell"><img
id="cellImage1-3" class="blank" data-x="1" data-y="3" src="css/
images/blank.png" data-bind="click: gameCellClicked"/></div>
        </div>
        <div id="row2" class="row col-xs-12">
            <div id="4" class="col-sm-offset-4 col-xs-1 game-
cell" ><img id="cellImage2-1" data-x="2" data-y="1" class="blank"
src="css/images/blank.png" data-bind="click: gameCellClicked"/></
div>
            <div id="5" class="col-xs-1 game-cell"><img
id="cellImage2-2" class="blank" data-x="2" data-y="2" src="css/
images/blank.png" data-bind="click: gameCellClicked"/></div>
            <div id="6" class="col-xs-1 game-cell"><img
id="cellImage2-3" class="blank" data-x="2" data-y="3" src="css/
images/blank.png" data-bind="click: gameCellClicked"/></div>
        </div>
        <div id="row3" class="row col-xs-12">
            <div id="7" class="col-sm-offset-4 col-xs-1 game-
cell"><img id="cellImage3-1" data-x="3" data-y="1" class="blank"
```

```
src="css/images/blank.png" data-bind="click: gameCellClicked"/></
div>
                <div id="8" class="col-xs-1 game-cell"><img
id="cellImage3-2" class="blank" data-x="3" data-y="2" src="css/
images/blank.png" data-bind="click: gameCellClicked"/></div>
                <div id="9" class="col-xs-1 game-cell"><img
id="cellImage3-3" class="blank" data-x="3" data-y="3" src="css/
images/blank.png" data-bind="click: gameCellClicked"/></div>
            </div>
        </div>
</section>

<footer>
    <div id="footerContent">
        <ul class="footerLinks" data-bind="foreach :
footerLinks">
            <li><a data-bind="text : name, attr : {id:
linkId, href : linkTarget}"></a></li>
        </ul>
        <span class="footerText">Copyright &copy; 2013. All
rights reserved.</span>
    </div>
</footer>
```

Let's take a look at the different sections of the code:

■ The first section of the code is the <header> element, which does exactly what its name suggests: it defines the header for the main game page.

■ The playing area is broken into two <section> elements. The first <section> element shows the current player information and any messages that may need to be displayed while the game is being played. The second <section> element is the game board itself. This is a nine-square grid (three columns by three rows) whose layout is managed by the CSS grid layout provided by Twitter Bootstrap. The key things to notice in the game board layout are that the x and y coordinates for each cell are being set as data attributes for the specific cell, and that a click binding has been set up for each cell using a Knockout data binding. Each cell also has a blank image set by default as a placeholder. The importance of the Knockout binding is that it allows us to do all of our WebSocket integration at the JavaScript layer and just assign the information that needs to be displayed in the game board, via Knockout's two-way binding mechanism. We do not have to set up any kind of event listeners on HTML DOM elements ourselves. All of that is handled by Knockout for us.

■ The last section is the <footer> element. It contains a list of links for the footer of our page. Again, Knockout is being used to dynamically provide the links themselves.

When the index.html file is loaded in the browser, each dependency is loaded in the order in which it's listed in the <head> section of the page. In the tictactoe.js file, there is a jQuery JavaScript call set up to bind the Knockout.js viewmodel to the view layer once the HTML page is fully loaded. Listing 4-6 shows this code.

Listing 4-6 *Knockout.js Binding*

```
vm = new boardViewModel();
$(document).ready(function() {
    ko.applyBindings(vm, document.getElementById('mainPage'));
});
```

When the Knockout binding is made, the viewmodel code is run. Not all browsers support the WebSocket protocol yet, so the first thing that you need to do in the viewmodel is make sure that your current browser does provide the proper support. For our example, this is achieved by using the code shown in Listing 4-7 from the tictactoe.js BoardViewModel() function.

Listing 4-7 *Checking for WebSocket Support*

```
if (typeof (websocket) !== "undefined") {
    ...
} else {
    alert('Websocket is NOT supported by your browser. Please use
a more modern browser to play this game.');
}
```

If the browser doesn't support the WebSocket protocol, this code will display an alert dialog that tells the player to use a more modern browser.

JavaScript API for WebSocket

You've learned about how to create and interact with the Java API for WebSocket on the server side, so now let's take a look at how that same WebSocket service can be consumed and interacted with from the client side.

WebSocket Initialization

When the `websocket.js` file is loaded, the initialization of the WebSocket connection is attempted as shown in Listing 4-8.

Listing 4-8 *WebSocket Endpoint Initialization*

```
var host = window.location.host;
var wsUri = "ws://" + host + "/TicTacToe/endpoint";
var websocket = new WebSocket(wsUri);
var output = document.getElementById("output");
```

You'll notice that the URL for the WebSocket endpoint is a reference to the endpoint that you set up during your work with the Java API for WebSocket.

While you can set the URL directly to the service in your final production code, it's a good idea to set up the URL dynamically when you are in development. The reason for this is more about testing than about development. When you run the code from the IDE, it will usually load with localhost as the hostname from your local development machine. However, if you hard-code the endpoint URL to localhost, you will have trouble connecting to the web application from some other device for testing. By getting the current hostname from the browser's window object, you can connect from any device on the same network for testing. As an example, if you run the tic-tac-toe game from your local machine, it will show up in the browser as `http://localhost:8080/TicTacToe/`. However, if you connected to the same web app from a tablet that is connected to the same wireless network, you would have to do something like `http://<ip address of dev machine>:8080/TicTacToe`.

Using the code shown in Listing 4-8 will connect using whichever hostname you join the game from.

WebSocket Control Methods

Just as when working with the Java API for WebSocket, you have five different methods available in the JavaScript API:

- `onopen()`

- `onmessage()`

- `onclose()`

- `onerror()`

- `send()`

As part of this sample application, an HTML element is set up to show the current state of the WebSocket connection. You can see this being defined as "output" in Listing 4-8. As you review the code for each of the JavaScript API methods shown in Listing 4-9, you will see that a function called `writeToScreen(message)` was defined as a simple means of setting the value for the output HTML element. The `onmessage()` method is not covered in Listing 4-9. It will be covered in a separate section after the other four methods.

Listing 4-9 *JavaScript Methods for WebSocket*

```
websocket.onopen = function() {
    displayMessage ("Connected!");
};
websocket.onclose = function(evt){
    var message = ' ';
    var closeCode = evt.code;
    if (closeCode == '1006'){
        message = "Error connecting to Websocket endpoint";
    }else if (closeCode == '1000'){
        message = "Connection closed normally";
    }else{
        message = "Closed with status: "+closeCode;
    }
    displayMessage (message);
};

websocket.onerror = function(evt) {
    displayMessage('<span style="color: red;">ERROR: </span> ' +
evt.data);
};

function send(text) {
    websocket.send(text);
}
```

Let's take a closer look at the methods shown in Listing 4-9. Remember that during the initialization, you defined the new WebSocket object as a variable named `websocket`.

- For `websocket.onopen(evt)` you are simply sending a message to the output variable saying that the connection was successful. This is the first event thrown by the WebSocket connection and is where you would do any additional setup code if you needed it.

- For `websocket.onclose(evt)` you are going to check for the code given by the WebSocket protocol to help determine why the connection was closed. The tricky part with doing this is that the WebSocket specification (RFC 6455) says only that the endpoint "may" send a close code, not that it has to. If a code is sent, it should conform with one of the close codes defined in the IETF specification (http://tools.ietf.org/html/rfc6455#section-7.4). The recommended codes are listed and described (quoting RFC 6455) in Table 4-1.

Code	Description
1000	Indicates a normal closure, meaning that the purpose for which the connection was established has been fulfilled.
1001	Indicates that an endpoint is "going away," such as a server going down or a browser having navigated away from a page.
1002	Indicates that an endpoint is terminating the connection due to a protocol error.
1003	Indicates that an endpoint is terminating the connection because it has received a type of data it cannot accept (e.g., an endpoint that understands only text data MAY send this if it receives a binary message).
1004	Reserved. The specific meaning might be defined in the future.
1005	Is a reserved value and MUST NOT be set as a status code in a Close control frame by an endpoint. It is designated for use in applications expecting a status code to indicate that no status code was actually present.

(Continued)

TABLE 4-1. *RFC 6455 Close Codes*

Code	Description
1006	Is a reserved value and MUST NOT be set as a status code in a Close control frame by an endpoint. It is designated for use in applications expecting a status code to indicate that the connection was closed abnormally (e.g., without sending or receiving a Close control frame).
1007	Indicates that an endpoint is terminating the connection because it has received data within a message that was not consistent with the type of the message (e.g., non-UTF-8 [RFC3629] data within a text message).
1008	Indicates that an endpoint is terminating the connection because it has received a message that violates its policy. This is a generic status code that can be returned when there is no other more suitable status code (e.g., 1003 or 1009) or if there is a need to hide specific details about the policy.
1009	Indicates that an endpoint is terminating the connection because it has received a message that is too big for it to process.
1010	Indicates that an endpoint (client) is terminating the connection because it has expected the server to negotiate one or more extensions, but the server didn't return them in the response message of the WebSocket handshake. The list of extensions that are needed SHOULD appear in the /reason/ part of the Close frame. Note that this status code is not used by the server, because it can fail the WebSocket handshake instead.
1011	Indicates that a server is terminating the connection because it encountered an unexpected condition that prevented it from fulfilling the request.
1015	Is a reserved value and MUST NOT be set as a status code in a Close control frame by an endpoint. It is designated for use in applications expecting a status code to indicate that the connection was closed due to a failure to perform a TLS handshake (e.g., the server certificate can't be verified).

TABLE 4-1.   *RFC 6455 Close Codes*

In the code for this game you are only going to check for a couple of specific codes, and just fall back to a generic message that shows the close code for anything else that may be sent by the endpoint. The check for close code 1006 is just in case the application tries to connect to the endpoint and it's not there. You can't use the `onerror()` event for this case because the WebSocket object is not completely created when this happens. It closes before it has been completely opened. The check for close code 1000 is to indicate that the New Game button was clicked and the `websocket.close()` method was called and processed successfully.

- The `websocket.onerror()` method is pretty self-explanatory. If there is an error, the endpoint may trigger an error event. That error would be captured by this method and the message will be displayed on the game.

- The `websocket.send()` method is used to send a message to the server. For this game example, only text is being sent and received over the WebSocket connection. However, the WebSocket protocol can also send and receive binary data in the form of a `Blob` or an `ArrayBuffer`.

WebSocket Data Management

The final method for the WebSocket API is `websocket.onmessage()`. This is where the heart of the communication between the client and server is performed. Listing 4-10 shows the code from the `websocket.js` file that handles the incoming text messages from the server endpoint.

Listing 4-10 *websocket.onmessage() Method*

```
websocket.onmessage = function(evt) {
    var json = null;
    try {
        json = $.parseJSON(evt.data);
    } catch (ex) {
        json = null;
    }
    if (json === null) {
        if (evt.data.toLowerCase().indexOf("x") >= 0) {
            vm.playerName('Player One');
            vm.showStatus(true);
```

```
                    vm.gameStatus('You Go First!');
                    vm.image(vm.X);
                    vm.symbol(vm.playerOne);
                } else {
                    vm.playerName('Player Two');
                    vm.showStatus(true);
                    vm.gameStatus('Please Wait');
                    vm.image(vm.O);
                    vm.symbol(vm.playerTwo);
                }
            } else {
                if (json.symbol === 'x') {
                    vm.image(vm.X);
                    vm.symbol(json.symbol);
                    setCellImage(json);
                } else {
                    vm.image(vm.O);
                    vm.symbol(json.symbol);
                    setCellImage(json);
                }
            }
        }
};
```

Let's walk through the code in Listing 4-10 to get a better idea of how the client interacts with the server for the game:

- The data that is being sent from the server is expected by the client to be in the form of a JSON object, except for the first time a browser connects. That first message is sent as plain text and indicates which player the game should be showing. Once the message is received, a try-catch block tries to parse the data from the event and assign it to the json variable. If this fails, then you know that this is the first connection for this player, and the json variable is set to null. If it succeeds, then the data is assigned to the variable and the game that is in progress can continue.

- The first time the browser connects to the WebSocket endpoint, the server sends back a message saying which player that connection is assigned to. Player X always goes first in the game of tic-tac-toe, so the retuned string is parsed for the character "x" and, if found, the onmessage() method does all of the game setup for "Player One." Any other connection string is assigned to "Player Two."

■ If the onmessage data is a JSON object, the symbol member of the object is checked to see if this is data for player X or player Y, and the onmessage() method sets the appropriate image name for that player. It then passes the JSON object over to the setCellImage() method for further processing. Figure 4-2 shows the use of the NetBeans IDE Network Monitor feature to see the data being sent and received in the WebSocket frame.

Managing the Game Logic

In the tictactoe.js file, the rest of the game logic is processed. Listing 4-11 shows the setCellImage() method.

Listing 4-11 *setCellImage() Method*

```
function setCellImage(data) {
    var myData = data;
    var cellId = "cellImage" + myData.x + "-" + myData.y;
    if (myData.symbol === 'x') {
        vm.image(vm.X);
        vm.symbol(vm.playerTwo);
    } else {
        vm.image(vm.O);
        vm.symbol(vm.playerOne);
    }
    $('#' + cellId).attr("src", vm.image());
    if (vm.gameStatus().toLowerCase().indexOf("wait") >= 0) {
        vm.gameStatus('Your turn');

    } else {
        vm.gameStatus('Please wait');

    }
}
```

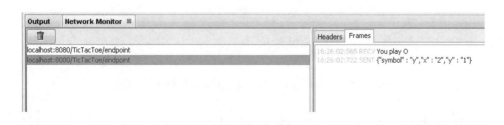

FIGURE 4-2. *NetBeans Network Monitor window*

When setting the image for the specific game cell, as shown in Listing 4-11, the image can be set either from the client of the player actually clicking the game cell or from the server to show what the opponent just selected. This method has to handle both cases. Here is where your use of the Knockout viewmodel starts to come into play. If the symbol member of the data object is for player X, the viewmodel's image attribute, or *observable* in Knockout terms, is set to be the image for X. You are then going to set the viewmodel's symbol observable to be the opposite of who just played. This is because the existing player's turn is done and you are beginning to set things up for the next player now. Next you set the src attribute of the specific cell to be that location of the X or Y image. Finally, the status needs to be updated to tell the players whose turn it is. If the gameStatus observable is currently set to "Please wait," then you switch it to say "Your turn." Otherwise, set it to "Please wait."

So far you have followed the flow of how things work when data is received from the server with the websocket.onmessage() event. The flow for clicking a specific game cell and then sending that data to the server and then your opponent is very similar, but it starts with the gameCellClicked() method shown in Listing 4-12.

Listing 4-12 *Capturing Game Cell Clicks and Sending Data*

```
function gameCellClicked(data, event) {
    var player = vm.symbol();
    var json = createJSON(player, $(event.currentTarget).
attr('data-x'), $(event.currentTarget).attr('data-y'));
    setCellImage(json);
    send(JSON.stringify(json));
}

function createJSON(symbol, x, y) {
    var jsonData = "{"
            + "\"symbol\" : \"" + symbol + "\","
            + "\"x\" : \"" + x + "\","
            + "\"y\" : \"" + y + "\"}";

    return JSON.parse(jsonData);
}
```

Let's walk through the two functions shown in Listing 4-12:

- When a cell on the game board is clicked, it calls the gameCellClicked() method. The Knockout click binding that is being used for this automatically sends the data and the event objects as part of the method. The data object in this case contains the current `boardViewModel()` content. The event object is what you are really looking for though. You want to know which game cell was clicked so you can set the appropriate image, and then you want to create the JSON data for that cell so you can send it back to the server and have your opponent's game board updated.

■ In the `gameCellClicked()` method, the current player is set by getting the value of `symbol` from the viewmodel. Then the values of the `data-x` and `data-y` attributes of the specific cell that was clicked are gathered. All three of these values are sent to a function that will format the values into the JSON object that your WebSocket endpoint expects. This is done in the `createJSON()` method shown in Listing 4-12.

NOTE
It would be desirable to use the HTML5 `dataset` method to get the `data-x` and `data-y` values in this function. If you were to use dataset, the code would look like this:

```
$(event.currentTarget).data('x')
```

The reason this is not done in this example is that the `dataset` HTML5 feature is not supported in all browsers at the time of writing. Internet Explorer specifically did not support this feature until IE 11 was released. Using a direct DOM call to get the attribute will work with all browsers.

■ The `createJSON()` function returns the formatted JSON as a JSON object so that it can be used in the `setCellImage()` function that you looked at earlier in Listing 4-11.

■ Once the image and game status have been set properly, the JSON object is converted back to a string so it can be sent to the WebSocket endpoint using the `websocket.send()` method. Remember that WebSocket data must be in either UTF-8 string format or a binary format of `Blob` or `ArrayBuffer`. Sending the actual JSON object will result in a WebSocket protocol error.

While the game code used for this chapter does not make use of the `Blob` or `ArrayBuffer` binary data types, you may want to know a little more about how they are used. `Blob` is the default binary data type, and there is nothing special that you have to do to send data in this format. Just pass in a `Blob` object as the argument to the `send()` method, just as you would with a text string. The server code will need to check for the type of the incoming message. Listing 4-13 shows a possible way of checking for the message type and processing it appropriately.

Listing 4-13 *Example of Testing for Message Type*

```
if (message.type === 'utf8') {
    console.log('Received Text Message: ' + message);
    ... // do something more with the string
}
else if (message.type === 'binary') {
    console.log('Received Binary Message: ' + message.binaryData.
length);
    ...  // do something more with the binary data
}
```

From the client side, you would need to provide some method for gathering the binary data and then passing that data to a function for processing and sending to the WebSocket connection. Listing 4-14 shows one possible solution: using an input type of `file` and allowing the end user to select a file and send it to the WebSocket stream.

Listing 4-14 *Example of Client-Side Code for Sending Binary Data*

```
document.getElementById("binary").addEventListener('change',
sendBinary, false);
function sendBinary(evt) {
    var file = evt.target.files[0];
    socket.binaryType = "arraybuffer";
    var reader = new FileReader();
    reader.readAsArrayBuffer(file);
    console.log('filesize: '+ file.size);
    reader.onload = function(e) {
        socket.send(e.target.result);
    };
}
```

Let's take a quick look at the code in Listing 4-14:

- The first line is adding an event listener to an input element of type file in the HTML markup. This input element has an id attribute set to the name "binary."

- When the event listener detects that a change has happened to the input element, it will call the `sendBinary()` function. This function uses the event object that the listener sent by default to get the file that the end user selected.

- The `sendBinary()` method then sets the `binaryType` property of the WebSocket connection to be a type of `ArrayBuffer`.

- At this point a `FileReader` object is created and the contents of the file are read into it using the `FileReader`'s `readAsArrayBuffer()` method.

- Finally, once the `FileReader` has completed the loading of the data, the data is sent over the WebSocket connection.

NOTE
It should be noted that the `FileReader` API is new to HTML5 and is not implemented by all browsers. Specifically, Internet Explorer 9 and any version of Safari older than 6.0 do not support it.

Summary

In this chapter you have learned about what the WebSocket protocol is, and how the APIs for both Java and JavaScript are used to interact with the WebSocket protocol on the server and in a pure client-side HTML5 application. You have learned how to work with the Java API for JSON to read and generate JSON objects on the server.

On the client side, you learned how to work with String and JSON object data to manipulate the HTML DOM elements and interact with the game board using the Knockout.js MVVM architectural pattern.

One thing that you may have noticed while either playing the game or reading all of the Knockout observables in the `boardViewModel()` is that there is not a scoring system implemented in the game. This omission is intentional. It is now up to you to take what you have learned and add the client- and server-side code that can store and manage the game state. The Knockout observables of win, lose, and tie are already in place and ready for you to use with the gameStatus system that is in place.

In Chapter 5 you will learn more details about working with HTML5, JavaScript, and CSS. The Knockout.js library will also be given more attention.

CHAPTER
5

HTML5, JavaScript, and CSS

The increase in development and availability of HTML5 applications for just about every type of device, from desktop computers to smartphones, and everything in between, has brought much-needed scrutiny to how HTML5 applications can best be used in the enterprise application space. In this chapter you will learn how to create a pure client-side HTML5 application that will consume and interact with the REST, Server-Sent Events (SSE), and WebSocket Java web services that you learned how to write in previous chapters. You will see how to implement the Model-View-ViewModel (MVVM) architecture pattern through the use of the JavaScript library Knockout.js. You will also be shown the basics of responsive design techniques using CSS3 media queries to dynamically change the UI layout when the application is displayed on devices of different sizes. Finally, you will be shown the basics of working with Syntactically Awesome StyleSheets (SASS) and the Sassy CSS (SCSS) syntax for managing more complex CSS file sets in an enterprise application.

HTML5 Project Setup

To get started, create a new HTML5 project using NetBeans IDE:

1. Choose File | New Project.

2. As shown next, select HTML5 in the Categories pane and then select HTML5 Application in the Projects pane. Click the Next button to enter details about your project.

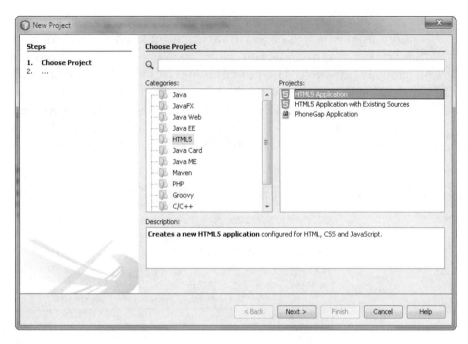

3. For the second step of the wizard, enter **BookClub** in the Project Name field and click Next again.

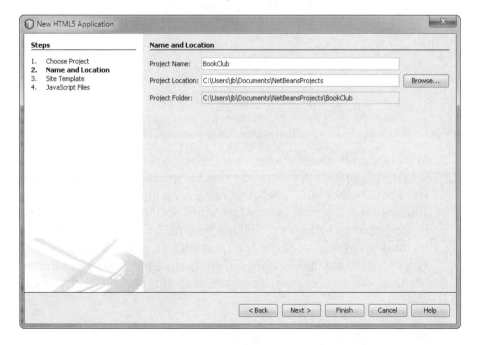

4. In the next step of the wizard, Site Template, you are given three options from which to choose how you want to configure your new project. For this example, you are going to base your new project on a template provided as part of this book. This template will provide the foundation for the information covered later in this chapter. So, as shown next, click the Select Template radio button, click the Browse button, and go to the location of the BookClub.zip file. Click the Next button after you have the BookClub.zip file selected in the Template field.

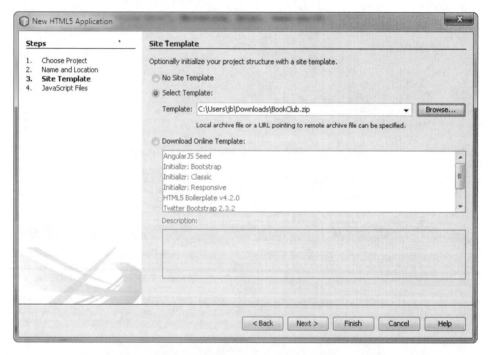

5. The last step in creating your new project is to add any other JavaScript libraries that you may need. The list of JavaScript libraries, shown partially in the following image, is pulled directly from the Content Delivery Network for JavaScript (CDNJS) repository and can be updated at any time by clicking the link under the library list. If you need to add more libraries at a later time, go to the Project Properties dialog in NetBeans IDE and select the JavaScript Library Manager option. For now, all of the JavaScript libraries that you will

need for this project are included in the template. Click the Finish
button to create the project.

Listing 5-1 shows the `index.html` file that the wizard loaded from
the template for your project. As you can see, the <title> element identifies
the name of your project. Also note how the CSS and JavaScript libraries
are referenced: The <link> and <script> tags in the <head> section tell the
browser to load the designated files when the `index.html` document
file is run.

Listing 5-1 *Setting Up CSS and JavaScript References*

```
<head>
  <title>My Book Club</title>
  <meta charset="UTF-8">
  <meta name="viewport" content="width=device-width">
  <link rel="stylesheet" href="css/bootstrap3/responsive.css"/>
  <script type="text/javascript" src="js/jquery/jquery.js"></
script>
```

```
  <script type="text/javascript" src="js/knockout/knockout-min.
js"></script>
  <script type="text/javascript" src="js/knockout.mapping/knockout.
mapping.js"></script>
  <script src="js/bootstrap3/bootstrap.js"></script>
  <script type="text/javascript" src="js/app.js"></script>
</head>
```

Notice that the last line of the <head> section includes an extra <script> element that references a JavaScript file called app.js. This file contains JavaScript code that is specific to this application. If you were starting this project from scratch and needed to add this file, you would right-click the js node in the project navigator, as shown here, and select New | JavaScript File.

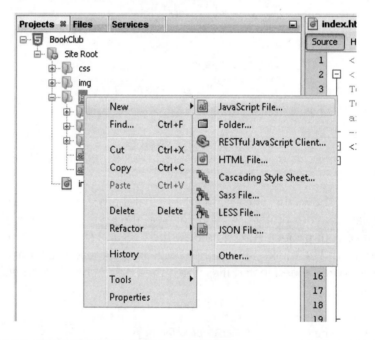

A dialog will be shown as in the following illustration. Set the file name to **app** and click Finish.

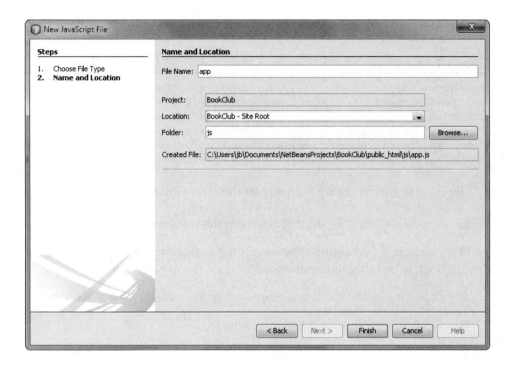

You can now run your project, and everything should load in the browser without errors.

REST

When working with a REST service, you first will want to identify the REST APIs that you have available to work with. This information is most often found in the developer documentation for the specific REST service. For this chapter, you are going to use the REST service and the persistence APIs that you created in Chapters 2 and 3 of this book. The code for those two chapters is available as part of the book for you to load and run from your installation of the NetBeans IDE. If you are running from a local machine, the URL will be `localhost:8080/sahara/webresources`.

The APIs that you have available are shown in Listing 5-2.

Listing 5-2 *Available REST APIs*

```
{hostname}/{application name}/webresources/books
{hostname}/{application name}/webresources/books/{id}
{hostname}/{application name}/webresources/books/{id}/authors
{hostname}/{application name}/webresources/authors
{hostname}/{application name}/webresources/authors/{id}
{hostname}/{application name}/webresources/authors/{id}/books
```

The APIs shown in Listing 5-2 provide the following functionality:

- /books returns a list of all books in the database.

- /books/{id} returns the details for a specific book. The {id} of a book is its ISBN (International Standard Book Number).

- /books/{id}/authors returns all of the authors for a specific book.

- /authors returns a list of all authors.

- /authors/{id} returns the details for a specific author. Each author has a unique ID in the database.

- /authors/{id}/books returns a list of all books that a specific author is associated with.

The easiest way to learn how to use a particular REST service is to write a CRUD application that exercises the APIs required to create, read, update, and delete data. You will use the APIs in Listing 5-2 to do just that in this section. All of the code discussed in this REST section is found in the app.js file of your project.

Read, Using the GET Request (R of CRUD)

You're going to start with the code shown in Listing 5-3 to perform a read of the available data.

Listing 5-3 *jQuery getJSON Method Call*

```
$.getJSON(self.serviceURL, function(data) {
    // do something with the data
});
```

This is a very simple call that uses the jQuery alias of $ and calls the .getJSON method. The call takes two arguments: the URL of the REST API, and a callback function to do something with the data that is returned. Listing 5-3 uses .getJSON() to make the call, so it requests the data to be returned as a JavaScript Object Notation (JSON) object. Because the JSON data format is syntactically identical to the code used to create JavaScript objects, it can be parsed directly from the JavaScript language without the need for any additional parsers or processors.

NOTE
$.getJSON *is a shortcut for*
```
$.ajax({
    type: "get",
    dataType: "json",
    url: url,
    data: data,
    success: success
});
```

You'll notice that the callback function only works against a successful request. If you need to do error handling, you will want to use the full syntax similar to what is shown in Listing 5-7 later in the chapter.

You'll also notice that the URL in this example is being set using a variable, self.serviceURL, instead of a string for the URL itself. This is because this line is actually part of a larger function called a ViewModel. This is part of the Knockout.js Model-View-ViewModel (MVVM) architectural pattern that you read about in Chapter 1. Listing 5-4 shows the full ViewModel code.

Listing 5-4 *Example ViewModel*

```
function booksViewModel() {
    var self = this;
    self.serviceURL = serviceRootURL + "/books";
    self.Books = ko.observableArray([]);
    $.getJSON(self.serviceURL, function(data) {
        var mappedBooks = $.map(data, function(item) {
            return new bookModel(item);
        });
        self.Books(mappedBooks);
    });
}
```

Let's walk through what each line provides:

- `function booksViewModel() { var self = this;` The current object in JavaScript is often referenced by a pseudo variable called `this`. The major problem with always using `this` to reference variables in a function is that the scope of `this` can change depending on how the function is called. You want to bind a local variable to the current `this` object so that the same object can still be referenced no matter how the function is called later in your code.

- `self.serviceURL = serviceRootURL + "/books";` This line sets up the URL that will be used to make the actual REST API call. Since all of the REST API calls have the same hostname and application path, a global variable has been set to contain the part of the URL that is always the same. One thing to keep in mind while working with REST service calls in development mode is that the hostname may vary as you test your code from different devices. For example, using "localhost" as the hostname will work fine for any browser that you would use to connect to the REST service that you have running on the same machine. However, if you were to try to test your code from, say, a tablet and connect to the IP address of your development machine, the JavaScript call to "localhost" would fail. For this reason, you will see at the top of the same application code that the `serviceHostname` variable is being set to `serviceHostname = window.location.hostname;` and the final `serviceRootURL` variable is created using this dynamic value.

  ```
  serviceHostname = window.location.hostname;
  ```

  ```
  serviceRootURL="http://"+serviceHostname+":8080/sahara/
  webresources";
  ```

- `self.Books = ko.observableArray([]);` This shows your first use of a Knockout.js method. You are assigning the variable `self.Books` to a Knockout observableArray and initializing it with an empty array. The use of Knockout observables and observableArrays is the key to setting up two-way binding between the data at the Model layer of your MVVM architecture and the View layer. You'll see a bit later in this chapter how this observableArray is used.

- ■ `$.getJSON(self.serviceURL, function(data) {`   This line was already presented in Listing 5-3 and discussed thereafter, but the variables should make a little more sense at this point. The callback function is processed when a successful request is returned. The `data` object contains the data that is returned from the server as part of the `response` object. Because you are using `$.getJSON()`, the data returned is a JSON object.

- ■ `var mappedBooks = $.map(data, function(item) {`   This line is using the jQuery `.map()` utility method to take each top-level element in the returned JSON object and add it to an array. Each item is created as a new `bookModel` object before it is returned from the `.map()` method.

- ■ `return new bookModel(item);`   In the end, you have an array that contains a collection of models. You'll find out more about the `Model` object when Listing 5-5 is discussed a bit later.

- ■ `self.Books(mappedBooks);`   This final line sets the value of the predefined observableArray `self.Books` to contain the collection of `Model` objects. You will see how this object is used when you bind the ViewModel to the View layer.

The Model represents one instance of your data. It's easiest to think of this as a single record in your database, or a single row of a table. In Listing 5-5 you can see that each field in your Model is assigned to a Knockout observable variable. This lets you take advantage of the two-way binding that Knockout.js is known for. *Two-way binding* means that when the value of an observable or observableArray is changed, either programmatically or from end-user data entry, the Knockout libraries automatically update all of the elements that are bound to it. You do not have to worry about setting up listeners for every variable that is used in your View layer. (This will become clearer when you get to the discussion of the View layer a little later in the chapter.) In the last line of the Model, you will notice that you not only assign each field from the data set, but you can also define your own variables that will be used in your View layer. In the example application, the book cover photos are provided already and are named after the ISBN code for each book. In Listing 5-5, you can see that the variable `this.coverImage` is being assigned to the value of `bookData.isbn` so that it can be used later to load that specific image in the HTML code.

Listing 5-5   *Example Model*

```
function bookModel(bookData) {
    this.description = ko.observable(bookData.description);
    this.isbn = ko.observable(bookData.isbn);
    this.publishedDate = ko.observable(formatDate(bookData.
publishedDate));
    this.publisher = ko.observable(bookData.publisher);
    this.title = ko.observable(bookData.title);
    this.coverImage = ko.observable(bookData.isbn);
}
```

Now that you have your Model and ViewModel created, there is one last piece to the puzzle. Listing 5-6 shows the HTML code for the View layer. This is included in the `main.html` file of your project.

Listing 5-6   *View Example*

```
<article id="bookInfo">
  <div class="item active" data-bind="foreach: Books ">
    <div id="bookCoverPhoto" class="bookCoverPhoto col-md-3" data-
bind="click: getBookDetails">
      <a class="thumbnail">
        <img alt="book cover photo" data-bind="attr: {src:
'img/'+coverImage()+'.jpg'}"  />
        <div class="caption" data-bind="text: title"
style="margin-left: 10px;"></div>
        <div id="isbnValue" class="hidden" data-bind="text:
isbn"></div>
      </a>
    </div>
  </div>
</article>
```

Let's break down this code example:

- `<article id="bookInfo">`   This element represents a simple semantic element that helps define the structure of the larger page. However, the `id` attribute is important because it is what will be used by the Knockout.js `applyBindings()` method to bind this section of the HTML View to the ViewModel that you created previously.

- `<div class="item active" data-bind="foreach: Books ">`   This line is the beginning of the list of books that will be rendered. This <div> will contain the layout and styling for one Model. If this were a table, this would be the layout and styling for one row of data. The key attribute is `data-bind`. This uses the Knockout `foreach:` binding to render everything contained inside this <div> for each item that is in the object "Books." Recall from the discussion about Listing 5-4 that you set the value of Books to the array of Models returned from the REST call.

■ `<div id="bookCoverPhoto" class="bookCoverPhoto col-md-3" data-bind="click: getBookDetails">` This <div> is the container for the book cover image and its caption. It has a Knockout `click:` binding bound to it so that you can drill down in your page to get more details about this specific book. You will see more about getting and displaying the book details a little later, as this details page will be used for the update and delete actions of your CRUD application.

■ The next three lines set up the contents that will be displayed for each book. The cover image, the caption, and the ISBN for each book are bound to their own HTML elements. There are two items of note in this code:

  ■ `data-bind="attr: {src: 'img/'+coverImage()+'. jpg'}"` In this `data-bind` attribute, the Knockout observable `coverImage` is being called as a method instead of just referencing the variable as you have seen done in all of the previous bindings so far. You do this when you want to get the actual value of the variable and not a reference to the function that Knockout uses for the two-way binding. This breaks the two-way binding for this reference, but in some cases, that is fine. In this case, you are just using the variable to dynamically get the name of the `coverImage` file. You do not plan on changing this name in other parts of your code, so you don't need to have it set up as a two-way binding. You will see a better example of why you would do this later in the chapter, when you get to the Update section of the code.

  ■ `class="hidden" data-bind="text: isbn">` In this code line, the value is being bound to the ISBN value for this particular book. You don't actually need to use this value as

Featured Books +

JavaScript: A Beginners Guide

HTML5 Multimedia Developers Guide

HTML5: A Beginners Guide

Java WebSockets Programming

FIGURE 5-1. *List of all books*

part of the current View, but you do need this value when you get the details for this book. By setting the CSS style `class` to `"hidden"`, the actual <div> is not rendered, but the ISBN value will be available as part of the data that Knockout passes to the function as part of the `click:` binding.

The final result of putting all of the code from Listing 5-3 through Listing 5-6 together will look like Figure 5-1 when you run it in a browser.

Create, Using the POST Request (C of CRUD)

Now that you know how to do the most common task, reading data, with a REST service, you will learn how to add a new record to your data service.

For this example, you will be adding a new book to the database. You will use the same REST API that you used for reading the list of books, `/books`; however, the request type that you use will be a POST request instead of the GET request that you used previously. Listing 5-7 shows the code for making this POST request.

Listing 5-7 *Example of AJAX POST Call*

```
$.ajax({
    url: serviceRootURL + "/books",
    type: 'POST',
    data: JSON.stringify(json),
    dataType: 'json',
    contentType: 'application/json',
```

```
    success: function(response, status, xhr) {
        booksVM.Books.push(new bookModel(json));
        $('#addBookDialog').modal('hide');
    },
    error: function(xhr, status, errorThrown){
        alert('Error adding new Book: '+status+": "+errorThrown)
    }
});
```

Let's walk through the code:

- $.ajax({, This is the jQuery method for implementing an asynchronous HTTP request (AJAX).

- url: serviceRootURL + "/books", This line sets the URL that you will make the REST call to.

- type: 'POST', This line sets the request type to POST. This tells the REST service that you want to add this new data to the database.

- data: JSON.stringify(json), The data that you will pass into the request is going to come from a form, which you'll learn how to create in a little while. Since the REST service is expecting to receive data as a JSON object, you will use the utility method .stringify() provided by the JSON object to convert the JavaScript object into a valid JSON object.

- dataType: 'json', This is the type of data that you are expecting back from the server in response to this request.

- contentType: 'application/json', This tells the server what type of data you are sending to it in this request.

- success: This is the callback function that is used if the request is successful.

- error: This the callback function that is used if the request fails.

TIP
To test your error callback function, try sending a request with the same value for a field that is required to be unique. In the case of the sample application, try adding two books with the same ISBN.

The HTML code shown in Listing 5-8 includes a Knockout `click:` binding that displays the dialog in which to enter the information about the new book that you want to add to the database.

Listing 5-8   *click: Binding to Show New Book Dialog*

```
<div id="featuredBooks" class="featured">
    Featured Books
    <span class="addNewBookIcon" data-bind="click: showAddDialog">
+ </span>
</div>
```

This code is straightforward. The Knockout `click:` binding is calling a function called `showAddDialog`. This function is using the modal dialog functionality provided by the Twitter Bootstrap framework (with which you initially created the project) to display a modal dialog. This dialog contains the form that gathers the details for new books being added to the database. Listing 5-9 shows the HTML for the dialog. The one line of code that displays the modal dialog is

```
$('#addBookDialog').modal('show');
```

Listing 5-9   *New Book Modal Dialog with Form*

```
<div id="addBookDialog" class="modal fade" tabindex="-1"
role="dialog" aria-labelledby="addBookLabel" aria-hidden="true">
<div class="modal-dialog">
    <div class="modal-content">
       <div class="modal-header">
          <button type="button" class="close" data-dismiss="modal"
aria-hidden="true"><img src="css/img/delete-16x16.png"/></button>
          <h3 id="addBookLabel"><strong>New Book</strong></h3>
       </div>
       <form class="form-horizontal" data-bind="submit: addBook">
          <div class="modal-body" style="padding: 20px;">
             <fieldset>
                <div class="form-group">
                   <label class="control-label col-md-3"
for="bookTitle">Title</label>
                   <div class="col-md-9">
                      <input id="bookTitle" type="text"
class="form-control"/>
                   </div>
                </div>
```

```
                <div class="form-group">
                    <label class="control-label col-md-3"
for="selectAuthor">Author</label>
                    <div class="col-md-9">
                        <select  id="selectAuthor" class="form-
control">
                            <option value="1">John Pollock</option>
                            <option value="2">Ken Bluttman</option>
                            <option value="3">Wendy Willard</option>
                            <option value="4">Danny Corward</option>
                        </select>
                    </div>
                </div>
                <div class="form-group">
                    <label class="control-label col-md-3"
for="bookISBN">ISBN</label>
                    <div class="col-md-9">
                        <input id="bookISBN" type="text" class="form-
control"/>
                    </div>
                </div>
                <div class="form-group">
                    <label class="control-label col-md-3"
for="bookPublisher">Publisher</label>
                    <div class="col-md-9">
                        <input id="bookPublisher" type="text"
class="form-control"/>
                    </div>
                </div>
                <div class="form-group">
                    <label class="control-label col-md-3" for="bookPu
blishedDate">Published</label>
                    <div class="col-md-9">
                        <input id="bookPublishedDate" type="text"
class="form-control" placeholder="mm-dd-yyyy" />
                    </div>
                </div>
                <div class="form-group">
                    <label class="control-label col-md-3"
for="bookCover">Cover Image</label>
                    <div class="col-md-9">
                        <input id="bookCover" type="file"
class="form-control" disabled="disabled" />
                    </div>
                </div>
                <div class="form-group">
                    <label class="control-label col-md-3"
for="bookDescrip">Description</label>
```

```
                    <div class="col-md-9">
                        <textarea id="bookDescrip" class="form-
control" rows="3"></textarea>
                    </div>
                </div>
            </fieldset>
        </div>
        <div class="modal-footer">
            <button class="btn btn-primary" type="submit">Save</
button>
            <button class="btn" data-dismiss="modal" aria-
hidden="true">Close</button>
        </div>
    </form>
</div>
</div>
</div>
```

This is a really large piece of code, but almost all of it is just HTML layout and styling. Let's discuss the lines that provide the functionality:

- `<form class="form-horizontal" data-bind="submit:`
  `addBook">` This is the Knockout `submit:` binding that tells
  Knockout to pass all of the form elements to the `addBook` function
  when a submit is performed.

- `<button class="btn btn-primary" type="submit">Save<`
  `/button>` By setting the `type` attribute of this button to
  `"submit"`, it will fire the submit event when it's clicked, causing the
  initial `submit:` binding to be invoked.

When the form is submitted, it will call back to the `addBook` function that contains the REST call that you reviewed previously. The only thing not shown in the previous example is how the data was formatted into the JSON object that was passed as part of the request. Listing 5-10 shows you how the JSON data is created using the form elements passed in by the Knockout `submit:` binding.

Listing 5-10   *Example Parsing Form Data to JSON Object*

```
function addBook(data) {
    var json = {
title: data.elements[1].value,
isbn: data.elements[3].value,
```

```
publisher: data.elements[4].value,
publishedDate: new Date(data.elements[5].value),
description: data.elements[7].value
};

...

}
```

The data passed into the `addBook()` function contains an array of the HTML elements, and you will assign the value, from those elements that you need, to the fields that are expected by the REST service. In this case, the array includes the five fields shown in Listing 5-10. When you are sending data to the REST service, you have to know in which format each field is expecting its value to be sent. For example, when the `publishedDate` field is being set, the REST service expects a `Date` to be sent for this field, so you will need to transform the data from the form into the appropriate format.

Data validation can be done in two ways at this point. You can use built-in validation functionality from the client-side frameworks, such as Twitter Bootstrap, to make sure that the data entered into the form is in the proper formats before the submit event is fired, and/or you can perform validation on the data as you are assigning it to the JSON object. The sample application provided doesn't perform any client-side validation. It does, however, provide a hint on the Published Date form field to help the end user know which format is expected for this field:

```
<input id="bookPublishedDate" type="text" class="form-control"
placeholder="mm-dd-yyyy" />
```

Knowing which specific HTML element contains the data that you want to assign to a specific field in your JSON object may be tricky if you have also included elements in your form that you don't want to use. NetBeans IDE provides a JavaScript debugger that is very useful for determining what is what in the data object returned to the function. Figure 5-2 shows an example of how the debugger can be used to determine which elements you need to use to achieve the code shown in Listing 5-10. Clicking in the left-hand gutter of your JavaScript file will place a breakpoint on that line, as shown for line 141 in Figure 5-2. When the form is submitted in the browser, the IDE will stop at this line. You can hover over the `data` variable to see the value of it in the tooltip. Expanding it will show each of the elements in the data object and their values. Of course, you can also see this debugger information in the Variables window at the bottom of the IDE if you don't want to use the tooltip approach.

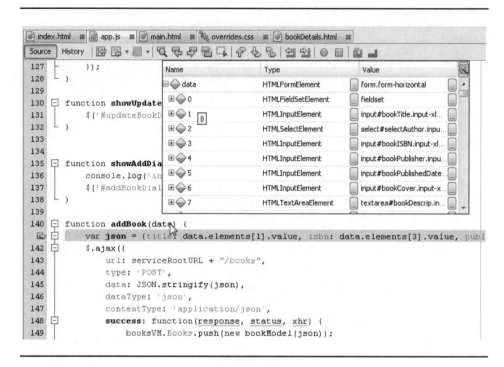

FIGURE 5-2. *NetBeans JavaScript debugger example*

Now that you have submitted the request to add the book to the REST service, you want to finish any changes to the View layer that may be affected by the result of the POST request. Taking another look at Listing 5-7, you will see the two callback functions for success and error. If there is an error, you should do something to inform the end user that the request didn't work. In this example, an alert is called with the error status and any text that the REST service returned as a result of the error:

```
error: function(xhr, status, errorThrown) {
    alert('Error adding new Book: ' + status + ": " + errorThrown);
}
```

In the case where the request is successful, you will want to add the same JSON data that you sent to the server to the existing Knockout observableArray that your View is bound to. In Listing 5-7, the line of code `booksVM.Books.push(new bookModel(json));` creates a new Model object out of the JSON data and then pushes it into the observableArray booksVM.Books(). Because Books is a Knockout observableArray, just adding the new Model object will cause an event to be fired, and the HTML that is bound to the foreach: binding will automatically update itself.

Update, Using the PUT Request (U of CRUD)

The process for updating a record is about the same as the process for creating a new entry, as covered in the previous section. First you will want to see the details for the book that you are going to edit. Listing 5-11 shows how the HTML is coded to list all of the books in your service.

Listing 5-11   *Example of Knockout foreach: Binding*

```
<div class="item active" data-bind="foreach: Books ">
    <div id="bookCoverPhoto" class="bookCoverPhoto col-md-3" data-
bind="click: getBookDetails">
        <a class="thumbnail">
            <img alt="book cover photo" data-bind="attr: {src:
'img/'+coverImage()+'.jpg'}"  />
            <div class="caption" data-bind="text: title"
style="margin-left: 10px;"></div>
            <div id="isbnValue" class="hidden" data-bind="text:
isbn"></div>
        </a>
    </div>
</div>
```

The Knockout binding of foreach: is used to display each item in Books with the same look and feel. Books is the Knockout observableArray from your ViewModel. The most important element in the HTML code is actually a hidden <div> that contains the ISBN for each book. The ISBN is a unique ID for each book, which will allow you to make another REST call to get the information about one specific book. Notice that each of the <div id="bookCoverPhoto"> elements for the book's cover image, title, and ISBN has a click: binding to the function getBookDetails(). This function will load the page that shows all the details about a specific book. Listing 5-12 shows this function.

▆▆▆▆ **Listing 5-12** *getBookDetails Function*

```
function getBookDetails(data) {
    var bookData = data;
    ko.cleanNode($('#mainPage'));
    $('#mainPage').load('bookDetails.html', function() {
        var vm = new bookDetailsViewModel(bookData);
        ko.applyBindings(vm, document.getElementById('bookInfo'));
        ko.applyBindings(vm, document.getElementById('bookDialogCon
tainer'));
    });
}
```

Let's take a look at this code:

- The first line simply sets a local variable, `bookData`, to contain the data from the page that you just left.

- The entire sample application that you have been working with so far is designed as a single-page application. This means that the application doesn't change URLs and load a new page when a request is made, but rather loads a new page fragment, or template, into a specific section of the larger page. In the case of this application, the `index.html` page has been designed to have the header and footer code and a single <div> in the body of the page to contain all the other page templates. This <div> has an ID of `mainpage`. Because Knockout allows you to have only one binding to a DOM element at one time, you need to clear out the existing binding and add the new bindings as you load the new page template.

- After `ko.cleanNode($('#mainPage'));` clears out the `mainpage` DOM element, `$('#mainPage').load ('bookDetails.html', function() {` loads the new page template into that same DOM element.

- In the callback function for the `.load` method, you will set the new ViewModel and bind that ViewModel to two separate DOM elements. The first is the container for all of the individual book details, and the second is the container for the modal dialogs. The dialogs will be used for updating the details for this book and as a confirmation of whether to delete the book or not.

Once you call the Knockout `applyBindings()` call, the
`bookDetailsViewModel()` ViewModel will be processed. Listing 5-13
shows this ViewModel code.

Listing 5-13 *Example of bookDetailsViewModel Function*

```
function bookDetailsViewModel(data) {
    var self = this;
    self.bookAuthor = ko.observable('');
    self.serviceURL = serviceRootURL + "/books/" + data.isbn() + "/
authors";
    self.isbn = ko.observable(data.isbn());
    self.publisher = ko.observable(data.publisher());
    self.publishedDate = ko.observable(data.publishedDate());
    self.title = ko.observable(data.title());
    self.description = ko.observable(data.description());
    $.getJSON(self.serviceURL, function(result) {
        if (result.length > 0) {
            self.bookAuthor(result[0].firstName + " " + result[0].
lastName);
        } else {
            self.bookAuthor("Unknown");
        }
    }, this);
}
```

When you created the new instance of the `bookDetailsViewModel()`
in the `getBookDetails()` function, you passed in the `bookData` variable.
This means that you have all of the information that you need for that specific
book and can assign those values to Knockout observables for use in your
View. However, the Author information is not included in that book data. The
Author details are kept in a separate table of your database. There is a REST
API for getting the Author details for a specific book, though. In the fourth
line of code in Listing 5-13, you can see that you are setting a variable called
`self.serviceURL` to point to that REST API.

Further down in Listing 5-13 you make a `getJSON()` call to get the
Author details:

```
$.getJSON(self.serviceURL, function(result)
```

In your database, Author is not a required field, so this API could return
successfully and still not contain specific information. Because of this, the

code is testing to see if the length of the returned data is larger than zero; if it is, the code sets the Knockout observable for the author's name to be a concatenation of the first and last name returned. If the returned data doesn't contain any information, the code sets the author to Unknown.

Now that you have loaded the new page template for book details and have pulled in the appropriate data to populate the page, you can take a look at how to allow your end user to edit the book data.

Listing 5-14 shows that at the top of the book details template HTML code there is a knockout `click:` binding added to an icon for Edit and another icon for Delete. Both of these functions do nothing more than load and display the dialogs for their specific purposes.

Listing 5-14   *Example of Icons for Edit and Delete*

```
<div id="bookTitle" class="bookTitle col-md-5" data-bind="text:
title">See Me Run</div>
<div class="bookTitle col-md-4">
  <img class="bookTitleAction" src="css/img/pencil-16x16.png" data-
bind="click: showUpdateDialog"/>
  <img class="bookTitleAction" src="css/img/delete-16x16.png" data-
bind="click: showDeleteDialog" />
</div>
```

Let's look at Listing 5-15 to see how the `updateBookDialog` dialog is handled first.

Listing 5-15   *Partial Edit Dialog*

```
<div id="updateBookDialog" class="modal fade" tabindex="-1"
role="dialog" aria-labelledby="updateBookLabel" aria-hidden="true">
<div class="modal-dialog">
    <div class="modal-content">
      <div class="modal-header">
          <button type="button" class="close" data-dismiss="modal"
aria-hidden="true">
                <img src="css/img/delete-16x16.png"/>
          </button>
          <h3 id="addBookLabel">Edit Book</h3>
      </div>
      <form id="updateForm" class="form-horizontal" data-
bind="submit: updateBook">
          <div class="modal-body">
            <fieldset>
```

```
                    <div class="form-group">
                        <label class="control-label col-md-3"
for="bookTitle">Title</label>
                        <div class="col-md-9">
                            <input id="bookTitle" type="text"
class="form-control" data-bind="value: title()"/>
                        </div>
                    </div>
                    <div class="form-group">
                        <label class="control-label col-md-3"
for="bookISBN">ISBN</label>
                        <div class="col-md-9">
                            <input id="bookISBN" type="text" class="form-
control" data-bind="value: isbn()"/>
                        </div>
                    </div>
```

Like the `addBookDialog` dialog created in Listing 5-9, this is a Twitter Bootstrap modal dialog. There are two important things to note in Listing 5-15. First, you don't need to pass in any information to this dialog directly. Each field is bound to the existing Knockout observable that was also used to display the book details in the main page.

NOTE

Notice that all <input> elements use a `value:` *binding while other DOM elements use a* `text:` *binding to get their content. When working with Knockout bindings, it's important to bind the proper content attribute for each type of DOM element. For example, if you set the content of a DOM element by using the* `value` *attribute, then you would use the value Knockout binding.*

Second, notice that the Knockout observables are being called as a function in all of the form element bindings: `data-bind="value: isbn()"`. This is very important. Because of Knockout's two-way binding, if you were to attempt a binding to the observable directly, as soon as you changed it in the form field, it would update in the book details page. You don't want this to happen immediately, just in case the end user clicks the Cancel button instead of submitting the changes. By calling the observable as a function, you get the actual value of the variable instead of the observable object.

Listing 5-16 shows how the form is processed and the actual update is performed in the REST API.

Listing 5-16 *Submitting Update*

```
function updateBook(data) {
    var json = {
        title: data.elements[1].value,
        isbn: data.elements[2].value,
        publisher: data.elements[3].value,
        publishedDate: new Date(data.elements[4].value),
        description: data.elements[5].value
    };
    $.ajax({
        url: serviceRootURL + "/books",
        type: 'PUT',
        data: JSON.stringify(json),
        dataType: 'json',
        contentType: 'application/json',
        success: function(data, status, xhr) {
            $('#updateBookDialog').modal('hide');
            $('#updateBookDialog').on('hidden.bs.modal', function()
{
                loadDefaults();
            });
        },
        error: function(xhr, status, errorThrown) {
            alert('Error updating the Book: ' + status + ": " +
errorThrown);
        }
    });
}
```

Let's walk through this code to examine what is going on:

- The JSON object that will be passed into the REST API call is being created using the form data passed when the Knockout `submit:` binding is triggered.

- The same AJAX call that you used to add a new book is used again to update a book. However, the `type` attribute used is now `PUT` instead of `POST` as was used for the add method.

- You have the same `success:` and `error:` callback functions as well. The `error:` function is exactly the same as before.

■ After the update has been completed, the application
  returns to the main page. The `success:` function closes the
  `updateBookDialog` dialog and then waits for that close to be
  completed. It then calls the `loadDefaults()` function, which
  resets the ViewModel and correct bindings back to the main page.

Delete, Using the DELETE Request (D of CRUD)

The setup for the update process was a little long, but that setup also enabled
the delete functionality. The `confirmDeleteDialog` dialog is displayed
in the same way that the `updateBookDialog` dialog was, with a call to a
`showDeleteDialog()` function. Listing 5-17 shows the REST API call that
is needed to perform a delete.

Listing 5-17 *Example of DELETE REST API Call*

```
function deleteBook(data) {
    var currentISBN = data.isbn();
    var books = booksVM.Books();

    $.ajax({
        url: serviceRootURL + "/books/" + data.isbn(),
        type: 'DELETE',
        dataType: 'json',
        contentType: 'application/json',
        success: function(data, status, xhr) {
          var match = ko.utils.arrayFirst(books, function(item) {
              return item.isbn() === currentISBN;
          });
          ko.utils.arrayRemoveItem(books, match);
          $('#confirmDeleteDialog').modal('hide');
          $('#confirmDeleteDialog').on('hidden.bs.modal',
function(){
                loadDefaults();
            });
        },
        error: function(xhr, status, errorThrown) {
            alert('Error deleting the Book: '+status+":
"+errorThrown);
        }
    })
}
```

After the user clicks the Yes button in the `confirmDeleteDialog` confirmation dialog, the `deleteBook(data)` function is called and the current `Books` details are passed to the function. To delete a record using a REST API, you need to have a unique ID for the record you want to delete. In the example application's case, this is the ISBN value.

Let's take a look at the code in Listing 5-17:

- The JSON object that will be passed to the AJAX call needs to contain only the unique ID for the record you want to delete. Notice that, once again, you are setting the actual value of the observable, and not a reference to the observable object.

- A local variable is set to the current ISBN value so that the ISBN value can be used in a comparison function later.

- A local variable is set to the `Books` observableArray so that you can remove the Model entry if the REST API call is successful.

- The URL is set in the AJAX call to use the REST API that will get the exact book that you want to delete.

- The `type` attribute is set to `DELETE`.

- The `dataType` and `contentType` are both set to JSON so that the service knows that is what you are sending and expecting back.

- As with all the other calls, there are `success:` and `error:` callback functions. The `error:` function is exactly the same as before.

- The `success:` function uses the Knockout utility function of `arrayFirst()` to find the first match in the observableArray. Once that is found, it returns a reference to that Model so that it can be removed using another Knockout utility function called `arrayRemoveItem()`.

- Just as you did with the `updateBookDialog` dialog, the `confirmDeleteDialog` dialog is closed, and then once the close is completed, the `loadDefaults()` function is called to reset the ViewModel and load the main page.

Server-Sent Events (SSE)

Server-Sent Events is sometimes referred to as *push* technology because the data flow is in one direction only. Everything comes from the server. The browser chooses to attach to the SSE stream to have information sent to it whenever new information becomes available. The example application has an Events section set up that will display data coming from an SSE stream. Knockout two-way binding is really helpful with the displaying of the data since you can set up the binding between the incoming data and a specific DOM element and just let Knockout update whenever the observable is changed by the new data coming in. Listing 5-18 shows how you connect to the SSE stream and which functions are used to work with the stream and its data.

Listing 5-18 *Example of Server-Sent Events*

```
function sseViewModel() {
    var self = this;
    self.sseData = ko.observable('test message');
    self.displayError = ko.observable(false);
    self.displayMessage = ko.observable(false);

    if (typeof (EventSource) !== "undefined") {
        self.source = new EventSource(serviceRootURL + "/books/
events");
        self.source.onopen = function(event) {
            var message = "SSE Connection Opened<hr>";
            self.sseData(message);
        };
        self.source.onmessage = function(event) {
            var message = self.sseData() + event.data +"<hr>";
            self.sseData(message);
        };
        self.source.onerror = function(event) {
            self.displayMessage(false);
            self.displayError(true);
            self.sseData(event.data);
        };
        self.displayMessage(true);
    } else {
        self.sseData("Sorry, your browser does not support server-
sent events...");
        self.displayError(true);
    }

    self.closeSSE = function() {
        self.source.close();
```

```
        self.sseData("SSE Connection Closed<hr>");
    };
}
```

Server-Sent Events is a new feature introduced in HTML5. Some browsers do not support this feature at the time of writing.

TIP

Currently, no versions of Microsoft Internet Explorer support Server-Sent Events.

Before continuing with the initialization code, it's a good idea to perform the following check to make sure the browser provides SSE support:

```
if (typeof (EventSource) !== "undefined") {
```

If the browser doesn't understand the type of EventSource, then it doesn't support SSE, in which case you can display an error message.

Let's walk through the code in Listing 5-18 to see what each section does:

- The first few lines set the defaults for your Knockout observables. These observables are bound to the SSE section of the HTML code.

- Inside the if statement that is checking to make sure the browser supports Server-Sent Events, you create a new EventSource object and assign it to the self.source variable. The URL that is used to make the connection is for the SSE stream that you wrote in Chapter 3 of the book:

```
new EventSource(serviceRootURL + "/books/events");
```

- Once you have the EventSource object, there are three events you can listen for and then perform the appropriate actions:

  - onopen: This event is triggered on the initial opening of the connection.

  - onmessage: This is triggered each time the server sends a message to the browser. This is the main event that you will want to work with.

  - onclose: This is triggered when the connection is closed for any reason.

■ In Listing 5-18, you are setting the local variable `message` to a string stating that the connection was opened. You are then assigning that value to the Knockout observable `sseData`, which will be displayed inside the SSE HTML section that is bound to the same observable. Because you are including HTML markup in the message, the Knockout binding on the HTML page is actually the `html:` binding instead of the plain `text:` binding:

```
<div id="sseMessage" data-bind="html: sseData, …</div>
```

■ In the `onmessage` function, you want to lay out the message that goes into this area by appending the most recent message from the server onto the end of the existing messages. You do this by setting the local variable `message` to the actual value of the observable and then appending the incoming `event.data`. After generating the new appended message, you set the `self.sseData` observable to the new value.

■ If the connection is closed for whatever reason, you set a message stating that the connection is closed and set the same `self.sseData` observable to show that message.

■ When the original observables for `self.displayMessage` and `self.displayError` were initialized, they were set to `false` so they would not show these areas while the page is loading. Now that the connection has been established and a message has been set, you can set the observable to `true`, which will display the Message area while still leaving the Error section hidden.

■ Finally, there is a small X icon in the View layer of the Event section that has been bound to the `closeSSE()` function. When the icon is clicked, the current SSE stream closes and an appropriate message is displayed.

WebSocket

Using the WebSocket API in JavaScript and connecting the resulting data to an HTML view layer was covered in Chapter 4. If you haven't read Chapter 4 yet, the basic approach to setting up the connection to the service is the same as what you just learned with Server-Sent Events. However, with the WebSocket API, you can also send data back to the server. One of the biggest advantages of using a WebSocket connection instead of REST or some other type of protocol is the significant reduction in the amount of traffic that you send over the wire when you use the WebSocket protocol. The connection between the client and server is set up once and then maintained until the connection is closed either via the API or via the client closing. With other protocols, you are required to go through the connection setup each time you want to send or receive data from the server.

To get a full description of the new WebSocket protocol, please read Chapter 4.

Responsive Design

The concept of responsive design addresses the need to design your web application such that it renders its layout appropriately in response to the screen size of the device on which it is being displayed. The application View layer needs to respond to this change in view size by changing the layout, or amount, of the content that is rendered.

The CSS2 specification provided the capability to use different CSS rules dynamically based on the media type. The most common of these types were (and continue to be in CSS3) screen and print. The CSS3 specification expands this capability with the introduction of *media queries*. A media query is made up of a media type and zero or more expressions. These expressions check for specific conditions of media features. A good example of this is an expression that checks for the current size of the display screen:

```
@media only screen and (min-width: 450px) and (max-width: 1024px){}
```

Through the use of media queries and a pattern of CSS classes defined as a grid layout, you can make your application respond to changes in the display screen.

The grid layout pattern is something that you can design yourself, but it's much easier to use an existing grid framework. Thus far, you have been using the Twitter Bootstrap framework to show modal dialogs and to help with the display of buttons and general form layout. Twitter Bootstrap also comes with a grid layout as part of its CSS files. The most common grid style in use is a 12-column grid. You can define different sections of your layout into any number of columns that would add up to the largest width of 12. For example, you could have three sections that were each set to be four columns wide. In the sample application's model dialog for adding a new book, for example, the dialog uses a nine-column width for all of the form elements, while the label elements use three columns. Listing 5-19 shows how this looks in part of that dialog HTML code.

Listing 5-19   *Sample Grid Layout HTML*

```
    <div class="form-group">
      <label class="control-label col-md-3" for="bookISBN">ISBN</
label>
      <div class="col-md-9">
          <input id="bookISBN" type="text" class="form-control"/>
      </div>
    </div>
    <div class="form-group">
      <label class="control-label col-md-3"
for="bookPublisher">Publisher</label>
      <div class="col-md-9">
          <input id="bookPublisher" type="text" class="form-
control"/>
      </div>
    </div>
```

Notice the style class of `class="col-md-9"` in each of the input `<div>` elements and the `class="col-md-3"` style class for the labels. The combination of these style classes and media queries is what makes responsive design possible.

Let's take a look at the CSS code in Listing 5-20.

Listing 5-20   *CSS Example for Grid Layout*

```
.col-md-9,
{
    position: relative;
    min-height: 1px;
    padding-right: 10px;
    padding-left: 10px;
}

@media (min-width: 992px) {
    .col-md-9
    {
        float: left;
    }

    .col-md-9 {
        width: 75%;
    }
}
```

The two sections of Listing 5-20 follow the style class for `.col-md-9` through to different media queries. The first section covers the situation in which the browser size doesn't fall into any specific defined media query. The second section introduces the media query for the situation in which the browser size is set to `min-width:992px`. Any style rules that you place inside a specific media query will override any previous values for the same rule while the media query expression is true. If you don't override a rule, the existing rule will continue to be used. In the code shown, you are not overriding an existing value, but rather setting new rules for `width:` and `float:`. Notice that the width is being set to a percentage instead of a specific numeric value. This will cause the nine-column grid to maintain its relative size as the browser is resized, but it still remains within the range that this media query has defined.

Figure 5-3 shows the CSS Styles property window in NetBeans IDE. Selecting an element in the DOM navigator will show that element's current CSS styles and rules, including whether the browser is currently resized to fit within a specific media query.

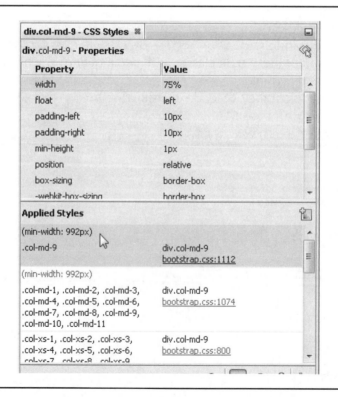

FIGURE 5-3. *NetBeans CSS Styles window*

Syntactically Awesome Stylesheets (SASS)

For most HTML5 applications, you may be able to get away with using a single CSS file that is reasonably constructed and easy to maintain. However, as the applications grow and become more complex, the CSS becomes just as complex. Historically, maintaining very large CSS files has been extremely difficult. Even if you broke the files down into smaller files and referenced each file in your HTML, you had to remember to place the files in the proper order because CSS files are loaded by the browser with the order they are listed, but each file will overwrite any previously set style classes. A concept of last in wins. If you happened to have the same rule defined in multiple files, the file in which the rule would take effect depended on the order in which the files were listed in your HTML code. In 2007, SASS was introduced by a developer named Hampton Catlin. The development of SASS is continued today by Nathan Weizenbaum and Chris Eppstein.

The original dynamic stylesheet language was designed to be similar to the Haml (HTML abstraction markup language) programming language in its use of an indentation syntax style. Referred to as *indented syntax*, this style really doesn't look or feel like CSS at all. This syntax is most often referenced with a file extension of .sass. A newer syntax has been created called Sassy CSS, or SCSS, which is designed to look and feel exactly like CSS itself—so much so that any valid CSS code is also a valid subset of SCSS. This syntax is most often referenced by a file extension of .scss.

SASS works as a preprocessor of the SASS or SCSS files and compiles these separate files into one or more CSS files that you can reference in your HTML code.

Listing 5-21 includes two link references to stylesheets. The first is for the Bootstrap framework that you used as the basis of the My Book Club sample application, and the second is the reference to the application's specific styles. The latter file, named `responsive.css`, is a CSS file that was generated as a result of the SASS preprocessing of four separate SCSS files. These files are shown in Figure 5-4.

Listing 5-21 *Referencing the CSS File*

```
<head>
    <title>My Book Club</title>
    <meta charset="UTF-8">
```

```
<meta name="viewport" content="width=device-width">
<link rel="stylesheet" href="css/bootstrap3/bootstrap.
css"/>
<link rel="stylesheet" href="css/responsive.css"/>
...
```

As you can see in Figure 5-4, the `responsive.scss` file contains only three lines of real code. It imports the other three SCSS files in the order in which you want them to be assembled. The other three files are broken out to contain the classes and rules specific to a certain media query type: in this case, Desktop, Tablet, and Handheld. This separation is just one example. Your individual projects will dictate how you determine what is the best way to break up your CSS into more manageable sections.

NetBeans IDE makes it very easy to work with SASS in your projects. Right-click your project name in the Navigator and select the Properties menu option. In the Project Properties dialog, select the CSS Preprocessors option, as shown in Figure 5-5. For this project, the IDE is being instructed to look for the SCSS files in a directory named `/scss` and to output the compiled files into the `/css` directory.

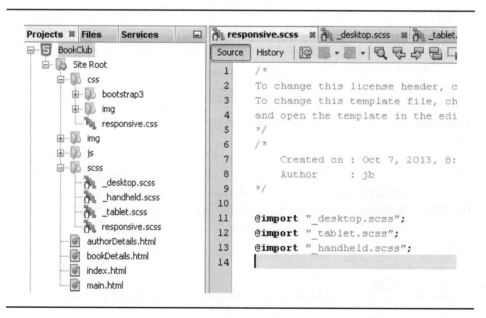

FIGURE 5-4. *Listing of SCSS and generated CSS files*

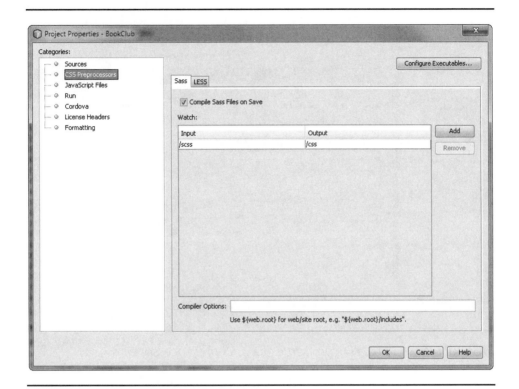

FIGURE 5-5.   *CSS preprocessor settings*

TIP
When working with SASS, if you start the name of an SCSS file with an underscore, that will instruct the compiler to not compile that specific file into its own CSS file. This is useful when you have multiple smaller files that are being imported into one larger file and you only want the larger file compiled to a final CSS file.

If you have not already done so, you can install and manage the executable for SASS by clicking the Configure Executables button at the top right of this dialog. The Global IDE options dialog for working with CSS preprocessor executables is shown in Figure 5-6. You'll notice that if you don't know where

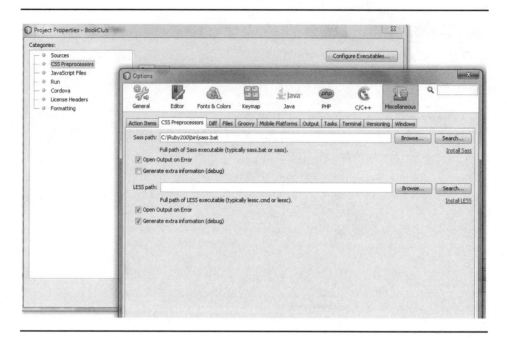

FIGURE 5-6. *Global IDE properties for CSS preprocessors*

to download the executable from, there is a link provided that will take you to the proper location.

You will also notice that NetBeans IDE supports another type of CSS preprocessing called LESS. This is a similar approach to SASS and was designed by Alexis Sellier in 2009. As with many open source projects, one project may influence another and vice versa. In this case, SASS was designed in 2007, which influenced the development of LESS in 2009. The introduction of LESS then influenced the new SCSS syntax used in SASS. Both stylesheet languages have their advantages and disadvantages. As far as NetBeans IDE is concerned, the setup and functionality are the same for either one.

Now that you have seen how you can work with SCSS files using NetBeans IDE, you are ready to take a look at the code. Listing 5-22 presents a very simple example of nesting, and then displays the resulting CSS in the generated file. All of the related rules for the `#footerContent` class are nested inside the root style in the SCSS file. After the CSS is compiled, the generated CSS contains separated rules.

Listing 5-22 *SCSS Nesting and the Resulting CSS Code*

```scss
#footerContent {
    float: left;
    ul {
        padding-left : 20px;
    }
    li {
        list-style: none;
        float : left;
        display : inline-block;
        margin-right: 5px;
        margin-left : 0px;
        padding-right : 5px;
        border-right : 1px solid #d9dfe3;
    }
    li:last-child {
        border-right : none;
    }
}

#footerContent {
    float: left;
}
#footerContent ul {
    padding-left: 20px;
}
#footerContent li {
    list-style: none;
    float: left;
    display: inline-block;
    margin-right: 5px;
    margin-left: 0px;
    padding-right: 5px;
    border-right: 1px solid #d9dfe3;
}
#footerContent li:last-child {
    border-right: none;
}
```

Summary

In this chapter you've learned how to work with an HTML5 project within NetBeans IDE and how to consume and interact with a REST web service to perform CRUD functions. You connected to a Server-Sent Events (SSE) stream using JavaScript, and then used the data from that stream to update an events window in the BookClub application. You were introduced to the Model-View-ViewModel (MVVM) architectural pattern through the use of the Knockout.js JavaScript library. You've also learned the basics of responsive design using a grid layout and media queries provided by the Twitter Bootstrap framework. Finally, you briefly looked at how you can use a CSS preprocessor to manage large and complex CSS implementations.

The BookClub application that was used throughout this chapter was intentionally left unfinished in the area of the Author details. This is so that you can use the tasks you learned while setting up the Book details to add the same type of functionality to the Author section of the application.

CHAPTER
6

HTML5 and Java
Application Security

A s an application developer, you may get the sense that every time you obtain a good understanding of the latest security issue, a new one crops up. Staying ahead of the security curve may seem practically impossible, but there are basic development practices that you can follow that will help you to at least keep up with the security curve. Application security can take many forms. In the case of HTML5 and Java web applications, the two major forms of security are client-side security and server-side security. The top issues and common best practices that apply to client-side security and server-side security differ, so this chapter discusses each separately, starting with securing the client side.

Client-Side Security

When working with HTML5 applications, always keep in mind this important fact: different HTTP traffic analyzers can read just about anything that you send or receive.

TIP
You should treat all data entering and exiting your HTML5 application as potentially malicious.

While almost all security measures need to be implemented on the server side for HTML5 applications, there are still a few types of client-side attacks that you need to be aware of, and properly code against, to avoid having your application exploited by hackers. These attack types include cross-site scripting, cross-site request forgery, and clickjacking. You will also want to have a basic understanding of authentication and authorization practices for your application and finally, some commonsense practices that should always be used when doing client-side security coding.

Cross-Site Scripting

Cross-site scripting (XSS) is one of the most common security vulnerabilities in web applications. There are actually three different kinds of XSS attacks: reflected, stored, and DOM-based. Reflected and stored XSS attacks are server-side attacks that must be handled at the application server or web server, whereas DOM-based XSS attacks are client-side attacks that must be addressed by client-side developers.

XSS occurs when a web application incorporates user input into the output that it generates without first properly validating or encoding the input. Data coming from the end user (for example, form input) or from a data connection (for example, a REST service) is considered untrusted data. You didn't create the data as part of your application, so you can't verify that it came from a trusted source. It's this untrusted data that you have to guard against.

The best way to understand XSS is to look at some examples. Although the focus of this section is client-side security, server-side XSS attacks are the easiest to understand, so a couple of examples of server-side XSS attacks are provided next, followed by a client-side example.

For the first example, assume that you've decided to create a custom error page for a 404 (file not found) error. When someone types in a URL similar to

```
http://my.website.com/not-here
```

the error page returns a message stating that the file `not-here` could not be found on the server. The XSS vulnerability occurs if the data displayed in the error message is not escaped properly before it's read by the browser, in which case an attacker could do something like this:

```
http://my.website.com/<script>alert("TEST");</script>
```

The browser would execute the <script> when it parsed the data to display it as part of the error message.

For the second example, assume that your web application has a search box. When a user conducts a search, the results of the search are displayed on a separate results page. The XSS vulnerability occurs if the results page uses the very common pattern of displaying "x number of results found for: <display what was searched for>" and does not perform proper encoding of the search string. If a malicious user enters a search string similar to the <script> block in the previous example, the JavaScript will be executed when the search results page is loaded in the browser.

Both of the preceding examples would normally be managed on the server side, because the error page and the search results page would normally be generated on the server. As previously mentioned, the third kind of XSS attack is purely client side and deals with how JavaScript handles the execution of DOM elements.

To demonstrate how a DOM-based XSS attack works, we'll use a similar example to the previous search field example. Suppose your HTML5 web application has a form that includes an input field requesting the user's username. The form also includes a <div> element that will be updated to show the content of whatever the user typed into the input field when the user presses the ENTER key. Listing 6-1 shows the code for this example.

Listing 6-1 *Form Example*

```
<label id="nameLbl" for="userName">User name: </label>
<input id="userName" autocomplete="off"/>

<div id="user"></div>
```

You want to set the contents of this <div> element to the value of the string entered into the `userName` input field. Doing this with plain JavaScript may look something like Listing 6-2.

Listing 6-2 *innerHTML Example*

```
document.getElementById("user").innerHTML = document.
getElementById("userName").value;
```

The code shown in Listing 6-2 will work just fine. However, by using the `.innerHTML` attribute of the <div> element, you have opened yourself up to a DOM-based XSS attack. If a malicious user were to enter a string that looked something like

```
<div onmouseover="javascript:alert('failed!')">XSS Test</div>
```

the HTML would be added to the DOM as written, and the next time someone moves their mouse over the new <div> element, the JavaScript would be executed.

There are certain DOM attributes and methods that you should avoid when working with untrusted data. A partial list includes

- `element.innerHTML`
- `document.write()`
- `document.writeln()`
- `javascript.eval()`
- element `eventHandlers`

- `.setTimeout`

- `.setInterval`

- `new function()`

In general, if you are working with untrusted data, set up your HTML so you can use the element's `.textContext` method, as shown in Listing 6-3, instead of trying to add HTML directly.

Listing 6-3   *textContext Example*

```
document.getElementById("user").textContext = document.
getElementById("userName").value;
```

If you absolutely have to allow untrusted data into a context that can be executed by either JavaScript or the HTML parser, then you should learn how to use one of the many HTML and JavaScript encoders that are available. You could try to write an encoder yourself, but doing so can be tricky because each browser's JavaScript engine can handle things a little bit differently. You are better off using an encoder that has been developed by a trusted security team, such as the Enterprise Security API (ESAPI) that is available from the Open Web Application Security Project (OWASP) team.

You should also be aware that using a JavaScript framework like jQuery poses the same issue. Using code such as

```
$('#user').html($('#userName').val());
```

will open the same XSS attack vector as using `.innerHTML`. If you are using jQuery, make sure you use `.text` instead of `.html`:

```
$('#user').text($('#userName').val());
```

NOTE
Modern versions of both Firefox and Chrome web browsers come equipped with a basic XSS auditor that will help prevent some kinds of XSS attacks. However, you should not rely on this functionality in any way as the sole method of protection. Using proper coding practices is the only way to truly protect against XSS attacks.

Cross-Site Request Forgery

Attacks that exploit the cross-site request forgery (CSRF) security vulnerability are uncommon because they are successful only under a very limited set of conditions. However, if you don't take some measures to guard against CSRF attacks, you are exposing your website visitors to a potentially very nasty result.

A good way to explain the CSRF attack is to use an example of a banking website. Let's call the website megabank.com. When you log into your account on this bank's website, the login stores a session cookie in your browser. This is a perfectly normal and acceptable practice for a banking website. The CSRF vulnerability exists if you leave the website without first logging out manually by clicking the Logout button. Your browser still has that session cookie in its cache up until the cookie expires. The expiration of the session cookie is set by the megabank.com website and in most cases will expire approximately 15 minutes after the last activity on the website. This expiration time can vary though. Suppose you next navigate to some other website that happens to have been hacked to include malicious code that, when activated (via a button click, for example), instructs your browser to send a request to megabank.com to transfer funds from "your" account to the hacker's account listed in the malicious code. When the megabank.com website receives the request, it will look for a session cookie to identify the user, which it will find in your browser because you just visited the website and didn't log out. The transfer will go through as if you performed the request yourself.

Although the chances are low that all the variables required for a successful CSRF attack will be present, it would take only one successful attack to ruin the reputation of the megabank.com website. If you've encountered spam emails or spam forum comment posts that just have links in them to some seemingly random websites, they could very well be attempts to lure you into a CSRF attack. The worst part of the CSRF vulnerability is that the end user doesn't even have to click anything on the website that is hacked. The entire attack can be handled via JavaScript when the page is loaded.

So, what can you do to help make sure your HTML5 application doesn't allow this kind of CSRF attack? First, be aware that your application has to be maintaining a session cookie in order for this type of attack to happen. If your application doesn't maintain session cookies (a stateless application), then it isn't vulnerable to this type of attack and you do not need to do anything. If your application does maintain session cookies, then your first priority is to make sure your website isn't susceptible to the XSS types of attack described in the previous section. If it is susceptible to XSS attacks, then anything you do to try and prevent CSRF attacks is meaningless.

To implement any kind of CSRF prevention in an HTML5 client-side application, you need to work in conjunction with what is being done on the server side of your application. The technique that you use to prevent CSRF is called double-sending cookies. This technique involves reading the session ID from the cookie that was sent from the server when the web page was first requested. Using JavaScript, you place that same session ID into a hidden field in all of the forms in your application, and attach it to any AJAX calls that your application makes back to the server. When sending the session ID value back to the server, it's often referred to as a CSRF token.

NOTE
Never set a CSRF token on an AJAX call that uses the method type of GET. Doing so will potentially expose the CSRF token in many different places (server logs, browser logs, network monitors, and so forth).

Using code similar to that shown in Listing 6-4 will allow you to echo the current session ID back to the server, which will then check to make sure that it matches the session ID in the cookie. Using this technique makes it extremely unlikely that the server will receive from another website a request that has both the proper session cookie and the same session ID in a hidden form element.

 Listing 6-4   *CSRF Hidden Form Token*

```
<form action="/servlet/formsubmission " method="post">
   <input type="hidden" name="CSRFToken" value="secret_key">
   …
</form>
<script>
   document.getElementById('csrf').setAttribute('value',
getCookie('Session'));
</script>
```

As you can see, the real solution to prevent CSRF attacks has to start at the server, but as a client-side developer, you can also do your part to protect against such attacks.

Clickjacking

Clickjacking is another type of attack against which you must protect your HTML5 web application. For a clickjacking attack to succeed, the attacker first must manage to wrap a web page from your application inside of a frame, or <iframe>, of some kind on a website that the hacker has created. The hacker creates a series of stacked transparent layers over the top of the website that the hacker created, which appears to be a normal website. When a website visitor thinks they are clicking buttons or links on this website, they are really interacting with your website and clicking a button or link that is not visible. Back in 2009, Chris Shiflett described an attack of this kind (http://shiflett.org/blog/2009/feb/twitter-dont-click-exploit) that used a Twitter page as the transparent overlay. When an end user clicked the visible "Don't Click" button, they were actually clicking the Post button of the hidden Twitter page and sending out a tweet devised by the attacker.

As with most of these kinds of attacks, the best way to defend against clickjacking is to do so from the server side. In the case of clickjacking, the service-side defense is to set the X-Frame-Options response header to either deny all types of frames or to allow only frames from the same domain. However, there is one coding practice that you can use on the client side to protect your application from clickjacking.

If you cannot modify the response headers from the server side, or you need to support older browser versions that don't understand the X-Frame-Options header, you can add the piece of code shown in Listing 6-5 to the <head> element of your pages to help protect against clickjacking attacks. This concept comes from Jason Li at Aspect Security and is discussed here: https://www.codemagi.com/blog/post/194.

Listing 6-5 *Anti-clickjacking Example*

```
<head>
<style id="antiClickjack">body{display:none !important;}</style>
<script type="text/javascript">
    if (self === top) {
        var antiClickjack = document.getElementById("antiClickj
ack");
        antiClickjack.parentNode.removeChild(antiClickjack);
    } else {
        top.location = self.location;
    }
</script>
...
</head>
```

Adding a `<style>` element to the top of your page enables the script that immediately follows it to know that it's referencing your page. If you were to use only the `else` part of the code by itself, the expression could be defeated through multiple kinds of workarounds. With the code in Listing 6-5, the script looks for the `antiClickjack` `<style>` element, and if it's not already the top layer, it moves it to the top. This is the OWASP-recommended method for preventing clickjacking attacks from the client side.

Authentication and Authorization

Probably the most obvious security issue when developing an HTML5 web application is how to handle your application login. None of the coding examples presented thus far in this book have included a login process, but if your application is going to store information that is specific to a user and/or information that will help to make the user's current visit to your application more enjoyable, then you will want to build some form of authentication into your application.

The most common method of authentication used for JavaScript applications is the OAuth standard. OAuth is an open standard for authentication. In 2006, a few developers from Twitter and Magnolia put together the concept for OAuth. Through the work of a small group of developers over the next year, a draft proposal for the OAuth standard was developed, resulting in a final draft that was released in October of 2007. In 2008, the OAuth specification was brought in front of a group of developers at the Internet Engineering Task Force (IETF) annual meeting for work on further standardization.

The OAuth 1.0 protocol was released in April 2010 as IETF RFC 5849 (http://tools.ietf.org/html/rfc5849). The OAuth standard is now the required authentication protocol for many leading web service APIs, such as Twitter, Flickr, Netflix, and others. The OAuth 2.0 specification was released as RFC 6749 (http://tools.ietf.org/html/rfc6749) in 2012. Although it is slowly gaining popularity across the Internet, many controversies arose throughout its development. Some of the original developers of the OAuth 1.0 protocol have resigned from the project because of disagreements over its direction and policies. To decide which of the two protocols to use in your specific situation, you will need to conduct further research on your own. It's safe to say that if your application needs to support direct authentication, you should start with the OAuth protocol.

Without getting into the technical details of the protocol, OAuth enables a client application, often a web application, to act on behalf of a user, with the user's permission. The main components of OAuth 2.0 are

- Client
- Authorization server
- Resource server
- Resource owner

The resource owner is an entity that can grant access to a protected resource. The client is the application that makes the access request on behalf of the resource owner. A client performs actions on a resource server based on authorization provided by the user at the authorization server. For example, a user can access images on www.flickr.com (resource server) via a web browser (client) by signing in to Flickr using their Google Account (where www.google .com is the authorization server). The advantage of this approach, as opposed to creating a separate login on www.flickr.com, is that the user does not have to create and remember multiple logins and passwords. Instead, the client obtains a *bearer token* from the authorization server, with the user's approval, and stores it. Then, when the resource needs to be accessed at the resource server, the client sends a special HTTP header in the following form:

```
Authorization: Bearer <token_value>
```

The token value is opaque to the client but can be decoded by a resource server so that the server can check that the client, on the user's behalf, has permission to access the resource.

If your application is going to be used as part of a larger enterprise environment that requires user authentication, then your application probably does not need to provide separate authentication. If you do need to include some form of authentication in your application, there are plenty of libraries in different languages by different authorization servers and resource providers that provide OAuth support. It's worth looking at them before deciding on your security infrastructure.

In a typical enterprise environment, your application will be part of a larger application server installation. This application server will do the authentication for your application, and the user will not get to your application's pages until they have already been authenticated by the application server's methods. This is also where the concept of authorization comes into play. Once the application server, or the identity management system that the application server is using, authenticates the end user, it can then be used to determine if the end user even has the rights, or is *authorized*, to access your application. In such an environment, you will need to get information from your security team about what kinds of checks your application will need to implement to make sure it behaves properly within your specific environment.

Client-Side Security Common Sense

A commonsense approach to client-side security will help you to avoid many pitfalls. With that in mind, here are some commonsense practices that you should consider following:

- Try to always run your application using the HTTPS protocol.

- If your application is running in a secure domain (HTTPS), don't connect your application to unsecured services. Make sure that your REST calls are also going to HTTPS domains and that your WebSocket calls are using wss instead of ws (see "WebSocket Security" later in the chapter).

- If at all possible, don't allow <script> elements in your HTML files. Place your JavaScript in external files and reference them.

- If you are using a JavaScript framework, check to see what kind of help it provides with common security issues, and use those features.

- Finally, take the time to research which security measures your specific application requires. You'll find that there is a lot of application security information available, and it's growing rapidly.

Server-Side Security

This section explains the key concepts of server-side security: authentication, authorization, confidentiality, and data integrity.

- Authentication validates the identity of a client. It determines whether the client is, in fact, really what it is claiming to be. It usually involves receiving a request from a client that includes a user

ID and credentials. The servlet container in a Java EE application server provides mechanisms to leverage standard web protocols and validate the credentials.

■ Authorization ensures that the authenticated client has appropriate rights to access the requested resource. This allows the server to check if the user can invoke certain operations on your service. The servlet container typically defines the operations that can be performed.

■ Confidentiality ensures that only the authorized recipients can access the information. This concept is similar to authorization, the key difference being that while authorization prevents the information from reaching unintended parties, confidentiality ensures that even if the information does reach unintended parties, it cannot be viewed or used.

■ Data integrity ensures that the information has not changed while in transit between the client and server. A hashcode, or signature of the data, is sent along with the data and confirmed on the receiving side.

Let's take a look at how these concepts can be realized in a Java EE container. After that, we'll turn our attention to REST resource security and WebSocket security.

Authentication

There are different ways to achieve authentication; the first two types listed next are from the RFC 2617 draft standard:

■ **Basic Authentication**   This is the simplest method of authentication over HTTP. The client, most often a web browser, opens a login box prompting the user to enter a username and password. The client then sends a base64-encoded username and password to the service. The server then checks if the user account exists and verifies the sent password. If the username and password match those of the account, then the resource is made available; otherwise, an HTTP 401 response code is returned to the client, informing the client that it is not authorized to access the resource.

Under the covers, the client generates an HTTP Authorization header set to a base64-encoded string of the username, a colon character, and the password. The authorization method and a space (that is, "Basic ") is added before this encoded string. If your username is "u1" and your password is "p1," then the header will look like this:

```
Authorization:Basic dTE6cDE=
```

Using Basic Authentication with HTTPS is highly recommended because otherwise the username and password can be easily decoded.

■ **Digest Authentication**   One of the limitations of Basic Authentication is that the password is sent in clear text and is susceptible to man-in-the-middle attacks. Digest Authentication, which is Basic Authentication over an encrypted HTTP connection, solves this problem.

Digest Authentication communicates credentials in an encrypted form by applying a hash function to the username, the password, a server-supplied nonce value, the HTTP method, and the requested URI.

For your username and password, the Authorization header looks like this:

```
Authorization: Digest username="u1",
    realm="file",
    nonce="o6mhNddONXUNMTM4NjgxMjQ1MTEzNfiTUvu5MR7R5KhM/wtvplE=",
    uri="/webresources/authors",
    algorithm=MD5,
    response="21c29c7a7c7600e5c39ba46637ad413a",
    opaque="000000000000000000000000000000000"
```

Many of the security options in Digest Authentication are optional so the server may operate in a security-reduced mode. Even though it is slightly better than Basic Authentication, it is still not intended to replace stronger authentication protocols, like client-cert. Like Basic Authentication, Digest Authentication is also susceptible to man-in-the-middle attacks. These types of attacks can be avoided by using HTTPS instead of HTTP.

■ **Form-based Authentication**   Form-based authentication allows customization of the login screen and error pages that are presented to the client. The contents of an HTML page for a login page should be coded as follows:

```
<form method="POST" action="j_security_check">
    Username: <input type="text" name="j_username"> <p/>
    Password: <input type="password" name="j_password"
autocomplete="off"> <p/>
    <input type="submit" value="Submit">
    <input type="reset" value="Reset">
</form>
```

The login form must contain fields for entering a username and a password. These fields must be named j_username and j_password, respectively. The action of the login form must be j_security_check.

The client is asked to enter the username and password and then click the Submit button, which submits the form to the server. If the authentication succeeds, the client is redirected to the requested resource. If the authentication fails, the error page is returned, which typically contains information about the failure.

■ **Client-Cert Authentication**   HTTPS not only provides a secure connection to the server but also can be used for authentication. This mechanism requires the client to possess a public key certificate (PKC) issued by a trusted organization, called a certificate authority. The PKC provides identification for the bearer. The server authenticates the client using this PKC.

The only disadvantage of this approach is the managing of the certificates themselves on both the client and server. Otherwise, this method is more secure than both Basic Authentication and form-based authentication.

All of these authentication mechanisms can be configured using the deployment descriptor (web.xml) of your application, as shown in Listing 6-6.

Listing 6-6   *Deployment Descriptor Example*

```
<web-app xmlns="http://xmlns.jcp.org/xml/ns/javaee"
        xmlns:xsi="http://www.w3.org/2001/XMLSchema-instance"
        xsi:schemaLocation="http://xmlns.jcp.org/xml/ns/javaee
http://xmlns.jcp.org/xml/ns/javaee/web-app_3_1.xsd"
        version="3.1">
```

```
<security-constraint>
    <web-resource-collection>
        <web-resource-name>Authors</web-resource-name>
        <url-pattern>/webresources/authors</url-pattern>
        <http-method>GET</http-method>
    </web-resource-collection>
    <auth-constraint>
        <role-name>admin</role-name>
    </auth-constraint>
</security-constraint>

<login-config>
    <auth-method>BASIC</auth-method>
    <realm-name>file</realm-name>
</login-config>

<security-role>
<role-name>admin</role-name>
</security-role>
</web-app>
```

As you can see in Listing 6-6, the deployment descriptor has three main elements:

■   The `<security-constraint>` element is used to associate security constraints with one or more web resource collections. It has the following subelements:

    ■   `<web-resource-collection>`   Identifies a subset of the resources and HTTP methods on those resources within a web application to which a security constraint applies. For example, in Listing 6-6, the security constraints are defined for the HTTP GET method on the resource accessible at `/webresources/authors`. Wildcards can be used to specify URL patterns, such as:

```
/webresources/*
/webresoures/authors/*
/*.html
```

    Once the user is authenticated, `<web-resource-collection>` defines which methods the user is authorized to access.

    ■   `<auth-constraint>`   Indicates the user roles that should be permitted access to this resource. The `<role-name>` used here must correspond to the `<role-name>` of one of the `<security-role>` elements defined for this web application. Alternatively, it can be the reserved role name, *, which indicates all roles in the web application. In other words, specifying the reserved role name * means that anybody who is able to log in can access the resource.

■ `<user-data-constraint>` If specified, indicates that the resources are accessible over a secure transport. In Listing 6-6, the following element would need to be added:

```
<user-data-constraint>
    <transport-guarantee>CONFIDENTIAL</transport-guarantee>
</user-data-constraint>
```

If a client tries to access the resource using HTTP, it is redirected to an HTTPS URL instead. This ensures that the data transmitted cannot be observed by other entities and thus allows enforcing of the key concept of confidentiality.

The `<transport-guarantee>` subelement can also take the value of NONE or INTEGRAL. The later value ensures that the data cannot be changed in transit and thus allows enforcing the key concept of data integrity.

It is also important to note that if one `<http-method>` is listed in `<security-constraint>`, then that method is protected as defined by the constraints in the deployment descriptor. All other HTTP methods not explicitly listed are called as *uncovered* methods. Adding a top-level `<deny-uncovered-http-methods/>` element to the deployment descriptor can protect these methods.

■ The `<login-config>` element is used to configure the authentication method and the realm name that should be used for this application. It has the following subelements:

■ `<auth-method>` Configures the authentication mechanism for the web application. The element content must be BASIC, DIGEST, FORM, CLIENT-CERT, or a vendor-specific authentication scheme. The first four values correspond to the different authentication schemes explained earlier.

- `<realm-name>`   Indicates the realm name to use for the authentication scheme chosen for the web application.

- The `<security-role>` element defines a security role. The subelement `<role-name>` designates the name of the security role. Note that these roles are created in an application server–specific way.

REST Resource Security

The following are some other guidelines to keep in mind when securing REST resources:

- Username and passwords, security tokens, or API keys should not appear in the URL, as these can be captured in web server logs and reused for malicious purposes.

- Every REST resource may not need to be read (GET), created (POST), updated (PUT), and deleted (DELETE). Make sure that only the required HTTP methods are exposed in the deployment descriptor and that other methods are explicitly protected using the mechanism defined earlier, such as `<deny-uncovered-http-methods/>`.

- Each user need not have access to all the REST resources. Use appropriate authorization by defining roles using `<security-role>` and giving access rights to resources accordingly using `<auth-constraint>`.

- For REST endpoints receiving multiple content types, always check the Content-Type header and use Bean Validation constraints, as discussed in Chapter 2, to restrict the types.

- Most third-party REST APIs allow authentication and authorization with popular OAuth providers like Google, Facebook, and Twitter. Consider integrating these providers instead of creating your own infrastructure from scratch.

WebSocket Security

WebSocket connections are upgraded from an existing HTTP connection. A plain WebSocket connection is established using the `ws` URI scheme, and a secure connection can be established using the `wss` URI scheme. This allows the WebSocket communication over standard ports 80 for plain text communication and 443 for secure communication, thus not requiring opening additional ports in firewalls. This also allows many existing HTTP security mechanisms to apply to a WebSocket connection.

WebSocket uses an origin-based security model policy commonly used by web browsers. RFC 6454 (www.ietf.org/rfc/rfc6454.txt) defines how user agents, such as browsers, isolate content retrieved from different origins (scheme, host, and port combination of the URL) to prevent malicious website operators from interfering with the operation of benign websites. Basically, content retrieved from one origin can interact freely with other content retrieved from that same origin, but it is restricted on how it can interact with content retrieved from a different origin. RFC 6454 defines an HTTP header field, named Origin, that indicates which origins are associated with an HTTP request. A WebSocket opening handshake from a browser is required to have this header so that subsequent requests can be serviced accordingly. However, this model does not work when a non-browser client initializes WebSocket connections.

In addition to the Origin field, the WebSocket opening handshake is required to have a Sec-WebSocket-Key field. This field is sent from the client as part of the opening handshake and is used by the server to prove that it received a valid WebSocket opening handshake. This helps to ensure that the server does not accept connections from non-WebSocket clients (for example, HTTP clients) that may be abused to send data to unsuspecting WebSocket servers.

As you can see, WebSocket already provides a decent level of protocol-level security. In addition, WebSocket endpoints within a Java EE application can be secured using the web container security model. A WebSocket mapped to a given `ws://` URI is protected in the deployment descriptor with a listing to an `http://` URI with the same hostname, port, and path since this is the URL of the opening handshake. A WebSocket application may use Basic Authentication or form-based authentication prior to the opening handshake. Similarly, WebSocket authorization may be set by adding a `<security-constraint>` element to the deployment descriptor. The `<url-pattern>` used in the security constraint is used to match the request URI of the opening handshake of WebSocket. Finally, a `<transport-guarantee>` of `CONFIDENTIAL` allows WebSocket communication over an encrypted `wss://` connection. This allows WebSocket applications to assign an authentication scheme, user roles, and a transport guarantee using standard mechanisms.

Summary

The HTML5 specification provides many new features that also bring their own potential security issues. While this book is focused specifically on HTML5 interactions with web services of REST, WebSocket, and Server-Sent Events, there may be other areas that you will want to research, such as local-storage, geolocation, and more.

The Open Web Application Security Project (OWASP) is a worldwide, not-for-profit organization whose main focus is on improving security in software. This organization's website (www.owasp.org) is a great resource for researching existing and potential security issues in all areas of HTML5 development.

Index

The Java User
Group Roundup
was great...

Can I copy Java
code to an HTML
extension?

Here's how I
use Oracle
JDeveloper...

I coded it
this way...

Did you sign up
for JavaOne yet?

How does
restricted task
reassignment
work?

I entered the
JavaOne Call for
Papers...

If you want to reformat
Java code to your code
style, try this method...

Where can I find
technical articles on
logging in Java ME?

Oracle Technology Network. It's code for sharing expertise.

Come to the best place to collaborate with other
IT professionals on everything Java.

Oracle Technology Network is the world's largest community
of developers, administrators, and architects using Java and other
industry-standard technologies with Oracle products.

Sign up for a free membership and you'll have access to:

- Discussion forums and hands-on labs
- Free downloadable software and sample code
- Product documentation
- Member-contributed content

Take advantage of our global network of knowledge.

JOIN TODAY ▷ Go to: oracle.com/technetwork/java

ORACLE®
TECHNOLOGY NETWORK

ORACLE®

Reach More than 700,000 Oracle Customers with Oracle Publishing Group

Connect with the Audience that Matters Most to Your Business

Oracle Magazine
The Largest IT Publication in the World
Circulation: 550,000
Audience: IT Managers, DBAs, Programmers, and Developers

Profit
Business Insight for Enterprise-Class Business Leaders to Help Them Build a Better Business Using Oracle Technology
Circulation: 100,000
Audience: Top Executives and Line of Business Managers

Java Magazine
The Essential Source on Java Technology, the Java Programming Language, and Java-Based Applications
Circulation: 125,000 and Growing Steady
Audience: Corporate and Independent Java Developers, Programmers, and Architects

For more information or to sign up for a FREE subscription:
Scan the QR code to visit Oracle Publishing online.